Tree Frogs

Complete Herp Care

Devin Edmonds

Tree Frogs

Project Team
Editor: Thomas Mazorlig
Copy Editor: Joann Woy
Cover Design: Mary Ann Kahn
Design: Mary Ann Kahn

T.F.H. Publications
President/CEO: Glen S. Axelrod
Executive Vice President: Mark E. Johnson
Publisher: Christopher T. Reggio
Production Manager: Kathy Bontz

T.F.H. Publications, Inc.
One TFH Plaza
Third and Union Avenues
Neptune City, NJ 07753

Printed and bound in China,
07 08 09 10 11   1 3 5 7 9 8 6 4 2

Library of Congress Cataloging-in-Publication Data
Edmonds, Devin.
    Tree frogs : a complete guide to arboreal amphibians / Devin Edmonds.
        p. cm.
    Includes bibliographical references and index.
    ISBN-13: 978-0-7938-2894-4 (alk. paper) 1. Hylidae. 2. Frogs as pets. I. Title.
SF459.F83E36 2007
639.3'7878--dc22
                                    2007019348

The Leader In Responsible Animal Care For Over 50 Years!®
www.tfh.com

Table of Contents

Chapter 1

Tree Frogs as Pets

Tree frogs are among the most interesting of amphibians, and some of the most popular to keep in captivity. Their agile behavior and charming appearance have captivated the interest of many people, from casual pet owners to professional herpetologists. Dozens of different species are available in the pet trade, providing a large variety of tree frogs to learn about and enjoy. Some are relatively low maintenance and make hardy captives, while other species are more difficult to keep and can be challenging for even the most experienced amphibian hobbyist or zoo keeper.

Natural History of Tree Frogs

As their name suggests, tree frogs are mainly arboreal, spending most of their time above ground on trees or other plants. To support this arboreal lifestyle, tree frogs have large, sticky toe pads that allow them to climb smooth surfaces, maneuver along thin branches, and scale flat rocks and plant leaves with ease. Nearly all species are nocturnal. This explains their greatly enlarged eyes, which help them see at night when they are active and give many an almost unworldly appearance, like something you could imagine beamed down from outer space. They are often heavily camouflaged to help them blend into their surroundings, whether lichen-covered bark or a large, uniformly green leaf. Not only are tree frogs camouflaged, but many species also possess the ability to change color depending on the environmental conditions to which they are exposed. Light levels, temperature, humidity, and their surroundings can all determine the color of a tree frog.

Many tree frogs have suction cup–like toes—such as those on this red-eyed tree frog—that allow them to cling to branches, leaves, and other surfaces.

Tree frogs occupy many different environments, from humid rainforests to hot, arid regions. Tree frogs live on all continents except Antarctica. The tropical rainforests of Central and South America are home to the greatest diversity of tree frog species, and contain nearly three-quarters of the large tree frog family Hylidae. Some tree frogs live exclusively in the canopy, never descending to ground level. Others tend to congregate around bodies of water, spending much of their time on emergent vegetation and small bushes or trees that surround ponds. Still others live in dry, desert regions, where they depend on unique adaptations to conserve water to survive.

As with all amphibians, water is critical for tree frogs and limits where they can be found. Some species utilize water-filled cavities in trees; others rely on streams or ponds. Rainfall is also an important water source for most tree frogs, and after a heavy rain many

Tree frogs depend on water to breed. Many species are seasonal breeders, and an increase in rain indicates that it's time to reproduce. Eggs can be laid in water or on floating plants, but they are also often deposited above water on leaves, or next to water on other vegetation, depending on the species. Tree frogs have an aquatic larval stage during which they are called tadpoles. Throughout this period they are fully aquatic, usually grazing on algae and detritus, until they metamorphose and leave the water. As tadpoles, tree frogs are very vulnerable to predators. Certain insects, insect larvae, fish, and even other tadpoles will eat them. Many tree frogs lay large numbers of eggs at one time to help ensure that at least some of their offspring survive past the larval stage.

Tree frogs use their enlarged eyes to locate food, relying on movement to catch their attention and initiate a feeding response. Live insects and other invertebrates are their preferred diet. Some larger tree frogs also feed on small lizards, and there are even species that specialize in feeding on other frogs. Small mammals and baby birds can be consumed by very large species.

Amphibian Population Declines

In recent years, many amphibians have undergone significant population declines, and a disturbing number of species have gone extinct. Numerous tree frog species are among the disappearing amphibians. One third of amphibians are threatened with extinction, according to the World Conservation Union.

Adaptable Desert Tree Frogs

Tree frogs are very diverse and even inhabit arid regions where water is scarce. In these areas, unique adaptations have evolved to help them conserve water. The casque-headed tree frog (*Triprion petasatus*) has an unusually flat head that it uses to plug the entrance of the holes in which it lives, thus preventing water loss and creating a humid place for it to spend the hot and often dry days. The waxy monkey tree frog (*Phyllomedusa sauvagii*) secretes a wax-like substance from glands. It covers itself in this wax during hot days to prevent desiccation.

The oddly shaped head of the casque-headed tree frog is a moisture-retaining adaptation.

One of the largest problems is habitat destruction. As the human population grows, more resources are used, often at a cost to the environment. Deforestation has caused problems for many species of amphibians that are unable to live in the plantations or bare

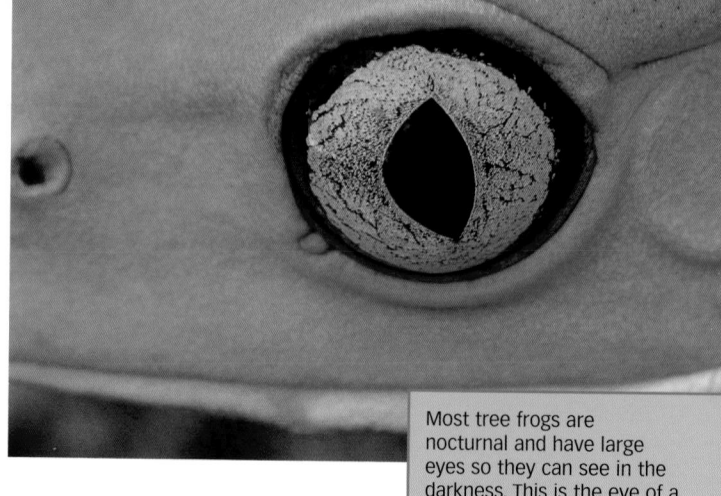

Most tree frogs are nocturnal and have large eyes so they can see in the darkness. This is the eye of a waxy monkey frog.

landscapes that remain after the forests are cut down. Wetlands, another important habitat for tree frogs, are also disappearing. Agricultural development has harmed many wetlands, as has the alteration of landscapes with dams and development projects such as subdivisions and business parks. Habitat protection and management are the solution to offsetting this damage.

Disease has also caused significant population declines. A particular fungus called *Batrachochytrium dendrobatidis* has decimated many amphibian populations, particularly those from cooler climates and higher altitudes where the fungus grows best. It belongs to a class of fungi commonly referred to as chytrids. These fungi are widespread, but until recently not known to infect vertebrates. The particular chytrid infecting amphibians has been linked to the extinction of multiple species and has wiped out numerous populations of tree frogs. Currently no solution is available to stop the spread of this devastating fungus in the wild, suggesting a grim fate for many of the world's most amazing frogs.

Taxonomy

The family Hylidae contains over 800 species of tree frogs. Organizing all these species into subfamilies and genera is a daunting task, and has been the work of many taxonomists. The most recent revision of Hylidae was published in 2005, in which the family was broken down into three subfamilies: Hylinae, Pelodryadinae, and Phyllomedusinae. The largest subfamily is Hylinae, in which nearly three-fourths of all hylids reside. Familiar tree frogs within Hylinae include the North American green tree frog (*Hyla cinerea*) and the Cuban tree frog (*Osteopilus septentrionalis*). The subfamily Pelodryadinae is restricted to Australia and surrounding islands. *Litoria* is the sole genus in Pelodryadinae, and within it is the commonly kept White's tree frog (*Litoria caerulea*). Phyllomedusinae has the fewest species of the three subfamilies, but contains some of the most sought-after tree frogs in the pet trade, including the red-eyed tree frog (*Agalychnis callidryas*) and waxy monkey frog (*Phyllomedusa sauvagii*).

Three other families, Arthroleptidae, Hyperoliidae, and Rhacophoridae, include certain arboreal species that many in the pet trade also commonly refer to as tree frogs, the key characteristic being enlarged toe pads and an arboreal lifestyle. Although not considered true tree frogs by some, they fit the description well enough to be included in this book. Arthroleptidae contains the African big-eyed tree frogs (*Leptopelis* species), which are sporadically available. The family Hyperoliidae is restricted to Africa and contains reed frogs (*Hyperolius* species), which are small, active, and commonly kept. The most familiar members of the family Rhacophoridae are Asian flying frogs (*Rhacophorus* species) and whipping tree frogs (*Polypedates* species), both living a highly arboreal lifestyle and being kept often in captivity.

Handling

For the most part, tree frogs are a look-but-don't-touch pet. They do not appreciate human interaction and perceive us as a threat, not a friend. Although a few species will tolerate occasional handling, most are best left in their cage. If you want a pet that can be handled, it might be best to avoid amphibians and instead look into some of the many reptiles available. Handling a tree frog can be harmful to them because they have sensitive,

Taxonomy Basics

A binomial ("two name") system is used to classify organisms, with each species name following the genus that organism is classified within. You can think of the *genus* as a big pot into which different individual species are sorted. These pots are then all kept in the kitchen, the *family*, which is inside of a house, the *order*, which belongs to a neighborhood, the *class*, and so on. Sometimes it is necessary to subdivide groups of species, and certain categories will be broken apart into subcategories, such as subfamilies.

Taxonomy of the red-eyed tree frog (*Agalychnis callidryas*) is as follows:

Kingdom: Animalia
Phylum: Chordata
Subphylum: Vertebrata
Class: Amphibia
Order: Anura

Family: Hylidae
Subfamily: Phyllomedusinae
Genus: *Agalychnis*
Species: *callidryas*

The reed frogs, such as the painted reed frog, are not considered true tree frogs, but they are similar in habits and captive care.

permeable skin that may be irritated by the oils and salts present on human hands. A moist net, cup, or other container can be used to catch or transport them. If a tree frog must be handled, the hands should be moist or wet to prevent causing harm.

Where to Purchase a Tree Frog

Tree frogs can be found for sale from a number of sources. Each has advantages and disadvantages.

Pet Stores

Pet stores offer a convenient location to acquire tree frogs. Many of the more common species can be found for sale, and pet stores that specialize in exotic pets usually offer a wide selection. Acquiring a tree frog from a pet store provides the opportunity to carefully inspect and observe not only the frog itself, but also the conditions in which it is being kept. Pet stores also offer a local place to ask questions and get help if the need arises. For this reason, it can be beneficial to develop a good relationship with some of the more knowledgeable staff at the store.

Herp Dealers

Your second option is to purchase tree frogs directly from dealers. These businesses specialize in selling reptiles and amphibians, and often are the source from which pet stores purchase their stock. They can be located on the Internet as well as in the classifieds section of certain pet magazines. Reptile and amphibian dealers usually offer significantly reduced prices compared to pet stores and also provide a greater selection. Unfortunately, these two advantages can be outweighed once the cost of shipping is factored in. In addition, some dealers may not offer much in the way of support or help to individuals who only purchase a few frogs, because most of their business is done on a larger scale, with pet stores and other dealers. Ordering from reptile and amphibian dealers is usually best when ordering a large number of frogs, as when developing a breeding project.

Breeders

Most tree frogs available are wild-caught, but a few species are regularly bred in captivity. Breeders offer quality animals at affordable prices and provide a reliable source for information. They are best located through the Internet. It can also be advantageous to contact a local herpetological club or society that may be able to direct you to a local breeder. Unfortunately, only a handful of species are bred in captivity consistently, so it may be difficult to find particular tree frogs from breeders.

Beginning tree frog keepers should start with a hardy species, such as White's tree frog.

Reptile Shows

You can also acquire tree frogs at reptile shows. These events offer a great opportunity not only to buy live reptiles, amphibians, and supplies, but also to have conversations with other people who share your interest. Dealers, breeders, and sometimes even specialty pet stores vend these events, combining all possible sources of tree frogs into one location. Many large reptile shows also have a series of lectures at which professionals speak about certain care techniques or experiences. Reptile shows are advertised on the Internet as well as in pet magazines.

Captive-Bred or Wild-Caught?

Wild-caught tree frogs are often subjected to fluctuating conditions during the trip from their origin to the seller, and they are not often cared for very well. Stress, bacterial infections, parasite problems, and abrasions from being overcrowded or housed in inadequate conditions are common health issues associated with wild-caught tree frogs. To help avoid these problems, try to purchase captive-bred tree frogs. When produced in captivity, frogs tend to be in better overall health and, for this reason, are much more desirable.

Unfortunately, many tree frogs are not consistently bred in captivity and are still heavily collected from the wild to supply the pet trade. When acquiring a wild-caught frog, it is especially important to carefully examine it for any possible health problems. You should

Scientific Names

Don't be afraid of scientific names. Although they may at first look overwhelming and difficult to pronounce, over time it becomes easier. Common names are unreliable, and the same name is often used for multiple species. For example, the common name "green tree frog" is used for both *Hyla* cinerea and *Litoria caerulea*, two species that require fairly different care. By using the scientific name, you can avoid confusing situations and mixing up different frogs.

also find out how long it has been in captivity. Those that have been in captivity for an extended time are usually less likely to do poorly than those that have just arrived at the pet store or dealer.

Selecting a Tree Frog

When choosing a tree frog, you may find many to select from, and some are usually in better shape than others. Understanding how to identify a healthy tree frog will help you choose an animal likely to provide years of enjoyment.

First, examine the frog's living conditions. Ensure that a source of clean water is available and that the substrate in the cage looks fresh, not old or waterlogged. Tree frogs housed in unhygienic conditions often develop health problems, such as bacterial infections, so if conditions are not sanitary, consider getting a tree frog from a different source. In addition, make note of how many frogs are housed together in the cage. Pet stores and dealers often stock tree frogs very heavily, which increases stress, so avoid tree frogs that are overcrowded. Also, determine if other reptiles or amphibians are being kept with the tree frogs. Tree frogs housed with other species may be exposed to diseases and parasites that are foreign to them, which could potentially cause problems.

Once a general inspection of the cage has been made, the next step is to examine the individual frogs. A healthy tree frog will be asleep during the day, unless food is available or they are disturbed. Most species should be perched somewhere above ground and not sitting on the floor of the cage. Ensure that the frog has good weight and does not look thin. Most tree frogs have a slightly round or plump appearance when perched asleep on the glass. Also, look closely at the eyes. Do not purchase any frog with cloudy eyes or those that look glazed over. To be safe, avoid frogs from any cage where other frogs housed with them have open soars, abrasions, or wounds, or otherwise look unhealthy.

Do not think that you must buy your tree frog a companion. Tree frogs do not need company in captivity and will be perfectly content kept alone.

Mixing Species

Housing different species of tree frogs together does not usually work for a number of reasons. First, few tree frogs require the same conditions in captivity, so the needs of one species must be compromised in order accommodate the needs of another. In the short term, this may work, but permanently housing tree frogs in improper conditions will lead to shortened lifespan. Second, when housing two different species together, you run the risk of exposing each to foreign pathogens, thus increasing the likelihood that they will get sick. Last, it isn't uncommon for one species to become food for another when there is a size difference between the two. Tree frogs are predators, a number of which feed on other frogs in the wild and won't hesitate to do so in captivity as well. Play it safe and keep different species in separate enclosures.

Bringing a Tree Frog Home

When transporting a tree frog, make certain that it is not exposed to extreme temperatures or other harmful conditions. Most often, amphibians are packaged in ventilated plastic cups when sold, but sometimes plastic bags are used instead. Place a slightly moist paper towel or damp moss inside the cup or bag. The temperature inside a bag or cup can change quickly, so it may need to be insulated to protect the tree frog it contains. On days when the weather is mild, a paper bag can be used as insulation, but in very hot or cold weather, a small cooler is best used.

Quarantine

All new tree frogs should be housed individually in a simple, hygienic setup for the first month or two while they are in your care. The quarantine period allows you to quickly recognize any developing problems and prevent the spread of disease to others. Resist all urges to handle a new tree frog in quarantine or wake them up simply to watch them. This can be stressful, and large amounts of stress can lead to a weakened immune system that allows health problems to develop. During the quarantine period, it can be useful to be in touch with a local veterinarian who has experience with amphibians, just in case any illness or health problem develops. Consider bringing a fecal sample to a vet during this period to have it examined for internal parasites, which often reach heightened levels while frogs are in the care of pet stores or dealers.

Chapter 2

Housing

lthough confusing to the novice, creating the proper environment for a tree frog is essential to good care, and it can be fun as you develop experience. Tree frogs need appropriate cages, substrates, water sources, furnishings, temperatures, and humidity levels to do well in captivity. A quick search on the Internet or trip to a few different pet stores will reveal many different opinions about the best way to provide all these housing requirements. My advice is to listen to all of them, sample a few different approaches, then determine what works best for both you and your frogs.

Tree frogs are a very diverse group of animals that live in a variety of environments, and not all species can be housed in the same manner. For this reason, it's important to research what type of setup is needed for the species of tree frog you plan to keep before setting up the cage.

Cages and Enclosures

During the day, tree frogs may appear motionless, but at night they awaken and actively move about. They are some of the most lively of all amphibians and need ample space to go about their business. Their powerful hind limbs can propel them long distances, so it's essential to offer horizontal space in addition to vertical room in which to climb. It's also important that the cage is easy to maintain because setups that are difficult to clean or access are likely to be neglected.

Glass Aquaria and Similar Enclosures

The most common type of enclosure used for tree frogs is the glass aquarium. These are available from most pet stores and come in a wide variety of shapes and sizes. Hexagon and "high" style aquariums work very well because they offer large areas of vertical space. Stagnant air can be problematic for many tree frogs, so always use a screen cover.

As an alternative to a standard aquarium, glass or acrylic cages designed for use with reptiles and amphibians can be used. These usually incorporate hinged or sliding front doors, which make it easy to access the inside of the cage. Reptile and amphibian cages also often have ventilation in the sides of the cage to help with air circulation. Both these features are desirable. These cages can be purchased at reptile shows and some specialty pet stores. Although they usually cost more than a standard aquarium, the price is generally worth it.

You can build your own front-opening cage for tree frogs by simply modifying an existing standard glass aquarium. By tipping a standard aquarium on its end, the height is increased. In this position, the opening of the aquarium is pointed to one side. A lip can then be created to hold the substrate in place by using aquarium-safe silicone sealant to secure a glass panel at the bottom of the opening (the original top of the aquarium). Above the glass panel, attach a door. Most often the door is made out of a frame and screen, to provide ventilation, and attached to the glass panel using silicone sealant and hinges. Position latches to secure the door in place.

Plastic Storage Containers

Large plastic storage containers are another option for housing tree frogs. They are a very practical way to keep frogs but need slight modification to serve as a permanent home. Ventilation is the main problem, but this can easily be remedied by drilling many small holes in the sides and cover of the container. Another option is to drill larger holes, measuring several inches in diameter, and attach aluminum window screening over the holes to prevent escapes. The two largest advantages to using plastic storage bins for housing are their low cost and light weight. Because they do not weigh as much as a standard glass aquarium or reptile cage, it's simple to bring a container to a sink and rinse it out to clean it. Unfortunately, the plastic used to manufacture most storage containers makes visibility poor.

To increase the vertical space of an aquarium, stand it on end and modify the opening to hold substrate.

Screen Cages

Screen or mesh cages can also be used to house some tree frogs. They work well for species that require a lot of ventilation or those that frequently damage their head by continually jumping into glass or acrylic. Use nonabrasive screen to avoid injuries. Screen cages made out of a soft mesh fabric, specifically designed to house reptiles and amphibians, are a better option than cages made out of window screen. It's important to note that crickets and other feeder insects are capable of chewing through certain types of mesh and screen. If a screen cage is used, it may be necessary to feed very small amounts frequently, to allow the frog to eat all insects quickly and prevent strays from chewing through the enclosure and escaping.

Custom-Made Enclosures

For very large tree frogs, you may want to build your own enclosure. Have glass cut to size by a glass shop, then fasten the pieces together using aquarium-safe silicone sealant. An easier method is to convert existing pieces of furniture into large tree frog enclosures. Shower stalls, large glass display cases, and other furniture can be modified by attaching glass, acrylic, or screen doors to already existing openings. Caulk the inside corners with silicone sealant and coat the sides with a waterproof epoxy that is safe for use with amphibians. When constructing your own cage for a tree frog, avoid using any material that is rough in texture or may be unsafe because of chemical treatments.

Substrate

The substrate is the bedding or material that goes on the bottom of the cage. Good substrates retain moisture, are easy to clean, and are either safe if accidentally ingested or too large for tree frogs to swallow.

Simple and Artificial Substrates

Paper Towel One of the most practical substrates available is paper toweling. When placed in layers on the bottom of the cage and moistened slightly, it forms a cheap, easily maintained, simple substrate.

Unfortunately, paper towels must be changed regularly to prevent the buildup of harmful bacteria, sometimes as often as once a day. For this reason, use them only in very simple enclosures that can be cleaned easily. They are the ideal substrate for temporary quarantine cages used when initially housing tree frogs.

Foam Rubber Upholstery foam rubber is another simple substrate that works well and is easy to clean. This material is sold at fabric stores for use as cushioning or padding. It comes in many different thicknesses; I prefer to use the $1/_2$- or 1-inch-thick (1.3 to 2.5 cm) material. Cut the foam rubber to fit the bottom of the cage and then moisten it. When soiled, it is easy to either replace the material or clean it with water. Cut holes in foam rubber for water dishes, perches, and other cage accessories so that these items sit flat on the bottom of the cage, making them more stable.

Damp paper towels make a simple and inexpensive substrate for many tree frogs, such as the Mexican leaf frog.

Bare Bottom The simplest of substrates is no substrate at all. Bare-bottom enclosures can be cleaned with ease, particularly if they are fitted with a drain. Using a bare bottom may not work well for all species, though, because the hard bottom of a cage can bruise and damage tree frogs when they lunge for prey. In addition, it may be difficult to maintain the proper levels of humidity without a substrate to retain moisture.

Reptile Carpeting Reptile cage carpeting or indoor/outdoor carpeting is often recommended as a good substrate for tree frogs, but I advise against it. Most cage carpeting is fairly abrasive and rough in texture. It does not hold moisture well, and requires frequent cleaning, which can be time-consuming when compared to the other simple substrates mentioned earlier.

Spot Removal

To remove water spots from old aquariums use white vinegar. After soaking the glass in vinegar, use a razor blade to scrape off the mineral deposits. Severe water spots from extended contact with hard water can etch the glass, which unfortunately cannot be removed.

Natural Substrates

Coconut Husk Fiber Ground coconut husk fiber is one of the most popular substrates for tree frogs. This material is made from hair-like fibers, called coir, that are extracted from the shells of coconuts. The fiber is then ground into a soil-like substance, dehydrated, and usually packaged in the form of a dry brick. When placed in water, this brick expands to several times its own size and turns back into the loose ground fiber. In this state, it resembles moist soil. Ground coconut husk fiber holds moisture well, is generally safe if accidentally swallowed by a frog, and is made in a sustainable way by using a byproduct produced when processing coconuts. It also provides the cage with an aesthetically pleasing, natural appearance, and it tends to hold up well, provided it does not become waterlogged. It is available at most pet stores.

A good way to determine how moist ground coconut husk fiber or soil should be is to take a handful and squeeze it. If it holds its form after being squeezed together, it is wet enough; if water oozes out, it is too wet for most tree frogs.

Soil A large selection of soils is available at garden centers and nurseries. Some work well as substrates for tree frogs, but others do not. Top soil is cheap and usable, provided it does not contain fertilizers, manure, or large amounts of rocks, clay, or sand. Potting soil should usually be avoided because most contain perlite, which sticks to tree frogs and can be irritating to them. Some potting soils also contain fertilizers or other chemicals that can harm amphibians. Peat moss is another soil-like product often encountered at garden centers. It is cheap and holds moisture well, both good qualities. Many mix it with other ingredients to form a soil mixture specifically for their amphibians. Unfortunately, most peat moss is harvested in a way that is damaging to bogs, which are unique environments that serve very important ecological roles. Ground coconut husk is a similar substrate that is harvested sustainably, making it a better choice.

Moss A few types of moss are available as substrate, one of which is an excellent choice for tree frogs. High-quality, long-fiber sphagnum moss can be found for sale at garden centers, and it works very well as a substrate because it is extremely absorbent. When you are ready to use it, soak it in water, then wring it out, leaving it slightly moist. Then place it in the cage and pat it down to form a flat, sponge-like substrate. Sphagnum moss should not be confused with the green moss sold at pet stores for reptiles and amphibians. This product can be used for aesthetic purposes and to add small areas of moisture or humidity, but it should not be used as the sole substrate.

Bark and Mulch Barks and mulches are sometimes recommended as substrates, but they can be problematic for a few reasons. The largest deterrent is that they can easily cause impactions if accidentally ingested by tree frogs. Fir bark, orchid bark, and other barks or mulches that can fit into a tree frog's mouth should not be used for this reason. Be sure to steer clear of mulch made from cedar or pine because the oils they contain irritate amphibians. Cypress mulch is one of the few types of mulch that has been used successfully as a substrate for tree frogs. It holds moisture well and is generally safe for frogs. Unfortunately, cypress mulch is manufactured by feeding young cypress trees into chippers, consequently destroying wetlands—ecosystems that are important to many wild amphibians. For the most part, other substrates make better choices.

Most tree frogs fare well on a substrate of moss. A Cuban tree frog is pictured here.

Gravel and Stones For many years, gravel was recommended as a substrate for frogs. Although gravel may work well for some aquatic amphibians, it can easily cause impactions if accidentally swallowed by a tree frog. For this reason, avoid using gravel as the sole substrate in the cage. Instead, use river rocks that are too large to be ingested by a frog. Do not use rocks that are sharp or have a rough surface. These could harm delicate amphibian skin.

Water Sources

Amphibians don't drink water as humans do. Instead, they absorb water through their permeable skin. To allow them to do this, it's important to provide a water dish for them to soak in. Simple water dishes include plastic deli cups or ceramic bowls. The smooth surfaces they contain make them easy to clean and allow for quick, trouble-free water changes. They are not pleasing to the eye though, and can look out of place in an elaborate, natural setup. As an alternative, purchase water dishes shaped to look like rocks or logs. Available at most pet stores, these are designed specifically for use with reptiles and amphibians.

Maintaining good water quality is essential to keeping tree frogs healthy. Most soak during the night, so make a habit of changing the water each morning. Do not use water straight from the tap to fill water dishes. Instead, use tap water that has been treated with a tap water conditioner that removes chlorine and chloramines and neutralizes heavy metals. As an alternative, bottled spring water can be used. Avoid bottled "drinking water" because it usually contains chlorine just like tap water. Some people prefer to create their own water for amphibians, starting with distilled or reverse-osmosis water. Reverse-osmosis water has been filtered through a membrane that allows only water molecules to pass, not impurities, and it is nearly as pure as distilled water. By adding aquarium products that contain essential salts and trace elements to these water sources, it is possible to create a safe water source for tree frogs.

Cage Furnishings

Most tree frogs need at least a few perches or branches to climb on. Driftwood works very well for this purpose. Pieces purchased from pet stores and labeled as safe for aquariums are good choices for tree frogs. Cork bark is another material that can be used to

Not All Frogs Can Swim

The sticky toe pads that tree frogs have are great for climbing, but not always useful for swimming. To make access in and out of a large water dish easier, place a gently sloping rock in the middle of it.

create climbing areas. It is sold in flat sheets, round tubes, and half tubes at many pet stores and some garden centers. Flat sheets can be wedged in place horizontally in the cage to create shelves or ledges. Use silicone sealant to glue pieces in place if necessary. Cork bark tubes are particularly useful and can serve as excellent arboreal hide spots for tree frogs. In simple cage setups, you can use plastic perches. Thin PVC piping can be cut to length and wedged in place horizontally in the cage, or larger diameters can simply be placed slanting in one corner to serve as both a perch and a hide spot. Artificial vines and branches make excellent climbing areas as well and can be found for sale in the reptile department of pet stores.

Silk or plastic plants can be used to create secure hiding areas for tree frogs. Many species appreciate vines draped along the sides of the tank to sleep behind during the day. Some tree frogs, such as the familiar red-eyed tree frog, do best in captivity when provided with large, broad-leaved plants on which to rest. Other small decorative plastic or silk plants can be used to make the tank look attractive. Avoid all artificial plants that have sharp points or edges.

Live plants can be used as an alternative to artificial ones provided a source of light is available for them. Live plants can be kept in their pots and placed on top of simple substrates or buried and concealed within soils or moss. Choose species that are hardy and can support the weight of the tree frog you're keeping. You may wish to rinse the plants off with water and grow them for several weeks outside of the enclosure to allow fertilizers and other chemicals to dissipate. See the terrarium plant chart included in this chapter for some recommended plants.

Cleaning and Maintenance

It's important to maintain a high level of cleanliness when keeping tree frogs. Spot clean the cage daily by removing feces and dead feeder insects from the substrate, sides of the cage, and cage furnishings. Wipe down the front of the cage once a week with a moist paper towel to maintain good visibility. Occasionally, completely clean the cage by changing the substrate and rinsing the cage and all furnishings with hot tap water. In small enclosures that are stocked heavily, this may need to be done as often as once a week. Larger enclosures that house only one or two tree frogs can go for longer periods of time between cleanings, sometimes even a few months if they are spot cleaned often. Never use soaps or household cleaners, because the residue left behind could harm tree frogs.

Temperature and Heating Devices

Different species of tree frogs require different temperatures. Some remain active and healthy even when temperatures drop into the 40°F range (4–9°C), while other species must be offered a very warm area in the cage that surpasses 90°F (32°C). Most captive tree frogs can be maintained somewhere between 70°F (21°C) and 85°F (29°C), but it's important to carefully research the temperature requirements of your particular species to determine a suitable range.

Use an accurate thermometer to measure the temperature. Digital ones with external probes are best and can be purchased at hardware and home supply stores. Plastic thermometers that suction-cup onto the side of the tank also work well. Avoid using the adhesive

As their name suggests, tree frogs require climbing branches in the cage. This is a White's tree frog.

thermometer strips designed for aquariums because these measure the temperature of the glass, which is not the temperature inside the cage.

You have a number of choices available if you need to provide heat in the enclosure. I prefer to use incandescent light bulbs. Pet stores sell many different styles of light bulb. What's important is not necessarily the kind of light bulb, but how powerful it is. Those that are more powerful have a higher wattage and produce more heat. It may take some experimentation to determine what wattage light bulb is necessary but, in most situations, only very low-wattage light bulbs are required. At night, infrared light bulbs or those made from black glass can be used so that the light doesn't disturb the frog. In addition to providing heat, infrared and black light bulbs (not the same as fluorescent black lights) allow tree frogs to be observed at night when they are active.

Some people have had luck heating tree frog enclosures with reptile heat pads. I find they work well when natural substrates are used to buffer and disperse the heat they produce. Avoid using hot rocks or other unsafe heating devices designed for reptiles.

Humidity

Tree frogs often require higher levels of humidity than are found in the average house. To increase the humidity, a number of techniques can be used. The most effective method is to mist the cage with a spray bottle once a day. Restricting ventilation is another method to increase the humidity. Vents and screen covers can be partially sealed by taping plastic wrap over part of them. Although high humidity levels may be important for some species, providing good ventilation is often just as critical, and it can be difficult to find a compromise between limiting ventilation and providing good air circulation. It's better to keep tree frogs in a well-ventilated, somewhat dry cage than a humid one with stagnant air.

If you're having difficulty maintaining the proper humidity level in the cage, try switching to a substrate that retains moisture well. Ground coconut husk fiber and sphagnum moss are both absorbent, and these are good substrates to use when keeping species that require high levels of humidity. Enclosure humidity is measured using a humidity gauge, which is available at pet stores that sell herps.

Lighting

Most tree frogs need no other lighting than an incandescent light to heat the cage and indirect light from the surrounding room to simulate a natural photoperiod. This results in a practical, but often unattractive and dim enclosure. To make the cage look better, you may wish to run a fluorescent strip light across its length. In addition to improving the appearance, this light also allows you to grow live plants. An electrical timer can be used to control the duration of the lighting. This should range from 10 to 12 hours a day.

For many diurnal reptiles, a particular spectrum of ultraviolet radiation, UVB, plays a large role in their ability to process calcium. Some have suggested that this UVB is also beneficial for many tree frogs, particularly species that sit exposed to the sun for long periods of time each day. It's been proved that tree frogs can live long lives in captivity without the use of bulbs that emit UVB. Nonetheless, many keepers still choose to use these bulbs for their tree frogs, and some attribute them to their success in maintaining particularly difficult species. If you choose to use a UVB-emitting light bulb, place it over a

Tree frogs can live in fairly simple enclosures as long as they provide all the frog's needs: shelter, warmth, humidity, and climbing areas.

screened section of the cage because glass and plastic filter out ultraviolet light. Always make sure your tree frogs have access to shaded hiding places so that they may escape the light when they wish.

The Living Terrarium

Over the last decade, keeping reptiles and amphibians in terrariums has increased substantially in popularity. In this approach, an attractive natural system is created in which live plants and beneficial microorganisms are used to help break down waste, limiting how often a cage must be cleaned. Terrariums take careful research and planning to create, but the rewards for housing tree frogs in them are great. A well-made terrarium is a creative way to bring the beauty of the natural world into your home.

Unfortunately, not all species of tree frogs are suitable for housing in such an environment. Large, heavy-bodied tree frogs should not be kept in terrariums because they are too messy, and their weight cannot be supported by most plants small enough to be grown in terrariums. Tree frogs that work well in terrariums are those that stay small, are from tropical or humid environments, and will not be destructive to plants.

Creating a Terrarium

To create a terrarium for tree frogs, first choose a suitable substrate. This serves both as a material for waste to collect on and as a medium in which to grow plants. I like to use a soil mixture largely based on ground coconut husk fiber, with milled sphagnum moss and fir bark mixed in. Sometimes leaf litter or leaf compost (usually oak or southern magnolia leaves), collected from a safe location, is also added. Other people have developed soil mixtures that contain different ingredients such as sand, coconut husk chunks, tree fern fiber, or peat moss. These soil components can be purchased at most garden centers and plant nurseries. Soil blends designed specifically for use in terrariums can also be purchased from specialty terrarium supply dealers on the Internet.

Do not use potting soil in terrariums because it breaks down quickly, and the perlite in it will stick to tree frogs, irritating them. To prevent soil from being ingested, it is helpful to place a layer of dried leaves over it. Collect these from a safe location where pesticides or fertilizers are not used.

Make sure the substrate remains well-drained to prevent plants from rotting. By raising the soil mixture above the bottom of the cage, excess water can drain through and collect below. One way to do this is to use a water-resistant drainage substrate below the soil. A layer of gravel is most often used as a drainage substrate. Place fiberglass window screening on top of the gravel to prevent the soil from mixing with it. Another popular drainage substrate is expanded clay aggregate, available from hydroponics supply companies. Often called LECA (lightweight expanded clay aggregate), it resembles brown, textured marbles. Expanded clay aggregate has the advantage of being significantly lighter than gravel.

An additional way to provide drainage is to create a false bottom. In this approach, egg-crate light reflective panels, undergravel filter plates, or other perforated plastic material is placed on legs (usually short segments of PVC pipe) and raised above the bottom of the tank. Fiberglass window screen is placed on top of the

A living terrarium set up by the author to house reed frogs.

perforated material, over which the soil mixture is placed. Water then drains through the soil and below the false bottom, preventing the soil from becoming waterlogged.

Set up a terrarium several weeks prior to housing frogs in it to let the plants grow in a bit and become established.

Backgrounds Prior to setting up the terrarium, you may wish to add a natural background to the inside of the cage. Cork bark flats work well they and can be attached to glass with silicone sealant.

A false bottom made of plastic egg-crate provides drainage in a living terrarium.

Stuff the gaps behind the cork bark full of sphagnum moss or fir bark to prevent feeder insects from hiding behind them. Tree fern panels are another good option for a background material. They can be purchased from orchid supply companies on the Internet as well as specialty greenhouses. Tree fern panels work well because they withstand moist conditions and have a dark, natural appearance, but they are often collected from forests in an unsustainable way, so consider their source prior to purchase.

Coconut fiber mats are another common background material. These are created from the same substance that ground coconut husk fiber is made from, but instead of grinding the coconut husk fiber into particles, the fibers are woven together and attached with an adhesive to form a mat. Coconut fiber mats are cheap, and they can be purchased at many garden centers and also from terrarium supply companies.

Plants Live plants define terrariums. They add an entirely new level of beauty to a tree frog habitat. Not only are they aesthetically pleasing, they also provide a service by using the waste produced by the frogs as fertilizer. Plants suitable for use in a terrarium can be purchased at plant nurseries and greenhouses, although many of the best species may only be found through special terrarium-plant dealers located on the Internet. Avoid any plant that has large spines or sharp stems or leaves, for obvious reasons. Also, ensure that the plants used do not outgrow your terrarium. Many common houseplants found for sale at garden centers quickly grow too large for the average tank, even with frequent pruning. Before using plants purchased from garden centers, wash them off under tap water, then repot them and grow them outside the terrarium for a couple weeks to allow any fertilizers, leaf shiners, or other chemicals to dissipate. Plants purchased from terrarium supply companies are usually grown without the use of harmful chemicals and can be planted directly into a terrarium.

Tree frogs themselves do not require any special lighting, but the plants used in a terrarium do. Using a standard fluorescent light bulb works fine for most common plant varieties. Using two or three bulbs works even better. I prefer to use fluorescent bulbs with a color spectrum between 5000K and 6500K because these produce a very natural white light. Special plant lights or "grow bulbs" can be used, but these give off an unnatural purple color. They are best used in conjunction with light bulbs that have a more natural color temperature. Compact fluorescent light bulbs are an alternative to standard fluorescent lighting, and produce much stronger light in a very efficient way. They are more expensive, though, and must be replaced annually.

Terrarium Maintenance

Although much of the waste generated in a terrarium is broken down by the bacteria and other organisms that live within it, work still must be done to maintain the living system. Spot clean to remove feces from the sides of the tank and plant leaves regularly. Use a damp paper towel and razor blade for this purpose, and avoid all chemical cleaners. Dead feeder insects are another form of waste that should be removed from the terrarium when noticed. The soil may need to be partially changed occasionally, but won't need to be entirely replaced unless it becomes waterlogged and spoils. Water will also periodically need to be drained from below the substrate. A siphon can be used to remove water from the drainage substrate, to prevent the water level from rising and saturating the soil. The plants in the terrarium will also require occasional maintenance. Pruning is necessary so that one species of plant doesn't shade out all the rest and take over the terrarium.

Another option for drainage is LECA (lightweight expanded clay aggregate), which is much more lightweight than gravel.

Plants Suitable for Tree Frog Terrariums

Scientific Name	Common Name	Comments
Aglaonema sp.	Chinese Evergreen	Will outgrow small terrariums
Alocasia sp	Elephant Ear	Attractive foliage, many will outgrow small terrariums
Anthurium sp.	Anthurium	Many species, most grow very large
Calathea sp.	Calathea	Leaves support tree frogs well, very hardy
Cryptanthus sp.	Earth Star	Needs well-drained soil
Ficus pumilia	Creeping Fig	Fast-growing vine, requires high humidity levels
Fittonia sp.	Polka-dot Plant	May be trampled by large tree frogs
Geogenanthus undatus		Strong leaves support small tree frogs well
Guzmania sp.	Bromeliad	Needs well-drained soil or may be grown epiphytically
Maranta sp.	Prayer plant	Prefers high humidity levels
Neoregelia sp.	Bromeliad	Needs well-drained soil or may be grown epiphytically
Pellionia pulchra	Satin Pellionia	Attractive, fast-growing plant
Pilea sp.	Aluminum Plant	May be trampled by large tree frogs, grows very fast
Philodendron sp.	Philodendron	Excellent terrarium plants, many species available
Sansevieria trifasciata	Snake Plant	Needs well-drained soil, strong vertical leaves form good perches
Scindapsus aureus	Pothos	Hardy plant that grows quickly, but can be kept pruned to fit the terrarium. Leaves are deep green in low light, or silvery/pale green in bright conditions.
Scindapsus pictus	Silver Vine	Attractive foliage, grows much slower than pothos. Fertilize every two months with a phosphorus-rich blend. Thrives in alkaline soil. Bright light.
Spathiphyllum sp	Peace Lily	Will outgrow small terrariums, good for a rain chamber
Syngonium podophyllum	Arrowhead Vine	Very hardy, grows quickly
Tradescantia fluminensis	Wandering Jew	May be trampled by large tree frogs
Vriesea sp.	Bromeliad	Needs well-drained soil or may be grown epiphytically

Chapter 3

Feeding

One of the most enjoyable aspects of keeping tree frogs is watching them eat. The suspenseful moment prior to the final lunge a tree frog takes at its food is something few keepers grow tired of, and the precision that many species exhibit when catching a meal is impressive to observe. The voracious appetite that drives this behavior is the reason many choose to keep tree frogs, and understanding their dietary requirements is important to successfully maintaining them in captivity.

Feeding

Nearly all tree frogs require live food. The movement of prey triggers the feeding response in amphibians, so pre-killed food is not usually an option. Occasionally, some tree frogs will accept freeze-dried insects from forceps, but for most it is necessary to offer live food. Feeding at night is preferable because this is when tree frogs are active and hunting, although many species can be conditioned to feed during the day instead.

The frequency with which tree frogs are fed depends on many factors, such as the age of the frog, what type of food is being offered, how much is being fed, and the species of frog being kept.

Young frogs grow best when fed daily or twice a day. Older adult frogs usually only require a feeding every 3 to 5 days. Adult frogs that are fed too often can easily become obese, which is one of the most common health problems affecting captive tree frogs. Tree frogs rely on instinct to catch food and will not stop feeding if they get full, so although most would gladly accept large amounts of food on a daily basis, it's much better to feed less frequently to avoid obesity.

The large eyes of tree frogs, demonstrated here on a tiger-legged monkey frog, enable them to track the movements of their prey at night.

A varied diet is the key to success. No one food can meet all a tree frog's nutritional requirements. Crickets should make up the majority of their diet, but other feeders must be substituted for crickets every few feedings. Offering three to eight crickets per frog per feeding usually works well, although this might need to be adjusted depending on the individual frog being fed. Other food items should be alternated every few feedings to add variety. If uneaten feeder insects are roaming the cage a few hours after feeding, the frogs are likely being overfed.

Not only is it important to provide a good diet for your tree frogs, it's also necessary to provide a good diet for their food as well. Feeder insects have often been starved or fed food that has little nutritional value prior to arriving in your care. To counter this, keep the feeders for a few days before feeding them to your frogs. During this time, offer plenty of nutritious food to restore their calorie content and increase their nutritional value. The food you offer to feeder insects must vary by species. More information on this topic is covered later in the chapter.

Supplementation

Understanding amphibian nutrition is complicated, and there are still many unanswered questions about their nutritional requirements. It is impossible to offer the variety of insects eaten by wild tree frogs to those in captivity, so to make up for the lack of diversity we must provide supplements.

Two different supplements are required to keep tree frogs healthy and prevent nutritional deficiencies. One should contain calcium and vitamin D3; the other should be a multi-vitamin supplement. Both of these generally come in a very fine powder, used to coat food items in prior to feeding. This is often referred to as dusting the food. Many different brands of supplements are available from pet stores, and not all are equal in terms of quality. Choose supplements that have an expiration date printed on their label because these will usually be of a higher quality than those without.

Unfortunately, it isn't possible to know how much supplement is ingested by a tree frog because we can't measure exactly how much is on each feeder insect when it is consumed.

In addition, feeder insects often groom themselves, thus removing some of a supplement before they are eaten. This prevents all of it from transferring to the tree frog. This can make it hard to determine how frequently a supplement should be used. For juvenile tree frogs, I like to alternate between a calcium and vitamin supplement at every feeding, only occasionally feeding without one of the two. When used at every feeding like this, the food should only be dusted lightly. Adult tree frogs can have their food items coated with supplements less frequently, sometimes as little as every third or fourth feeding.

Crickets

Crickets are the most common feeder insect used to feed tree frogs. They can be purchased from pet stores in small quantities or ordered in bulk from cricket breeders. Most

Gut-Loading

Gut-loading is a term used to describe feeding feeder insects food that is rich in certain vitamins or calcium so that these are then passed on to the animal that eats the insect. Many gut-loading diets are available from pet stores, but when used they sometimes result in a high mortality of feeder insects. For this reason, only use special gut-loading diets as they are intended, and feed the insects to your frogs within a few hours.

pet stores sell them in three sizes—small, medium, and large. Feed crickets that are about as long as the width of the frog's head. Crickets are easy to keep and a relatively healthy meal when they are well fed and coated in the appropriate vitamin and mineral supplement. They are an excellent feeder insect to make up the majority of a tree frog's diet.

Small numbers of crickets can be kept in aquariums or plastic cages. Larger numbers can be maintained in other containers, such as plastic storage bins or garbage cans. Crickets do best when kept warm, above 70°F (21°C), and they must have access to fresh food and water in order to survive. They are prone to drowning in water dishes, so provide water with a moist sponge. An even better way to provide moisture for crickets is to offer fresh fruits and vegetables as the only source of water, forcing the crickets to consume these vitamin-rich food items to stay hydrated. Oranges, apples, sweet potatoes, yams, carrots, squash, grapes, and dark green or red lettuces all can be used to provide both moisture and food. These should be sliced and placed onto a dish in the cricket's cage (for easy cleaning). In addition to fruits and vegetables, crickets should have access to dry food. Many good dry cricket diets are available from pet stores. As an alternative to commercial cricket diets, flake fish food, dry dog food, rice baby cereal, or oats can be used. Food should be replaced every other day or more often if it starts to go bad.

Feed crickets a nutritious diet, such as tropical fish flakes, before feeding them to your tree frogs.

Worms

Next to crickets, the most common food items available are what I like to call "worms." These include mealworms, super worms, wax worms, and silkworms, among others. These are not true annelids (e.g., earthworms) but are instead the larval form of particular insects. Worms should be offered at night so that they are eaten immediately; set them in a small dish to prevent them from crawling away and hiding in the substrate.

Silk worms are a highly nutritious insect to feed to your tree frogs.

Mealworms

Mealworms are the larval stage of darkling beetles (*Tenebrio* sp.). They can be purchased from both pet stores and live bait shops. Mealworms should be kept on bran, flour, or oats and provided with slices of sweet potato or other vegetable for moisture. They should be stored in the refrigerator to prevent them from pupating into beetles. Feed mealworms to tree frogs sparingly because they are high in fat, and their hard exoskeleton may be difficult for some frogs to digest.

Super Worms

Super worms, or king mealworms, are the larvae of another beetle belonging to the genus *Zophobas*. Because of their larger size, they are an excellent treat for large tree frogs. Like mealworms, super worms have a hard exoskeleton and are high in fat, so take care not to use them too frequently. Keep super worms at room temperature, but otherwise in the same manner as mealworms.

Wax Worms

The larvae of the greater wax moth (*Galleria mellonella*), usually called wax worms, are widely available from both pet stores and live bait shops. They lack the hard exoskeleton of mealworms and super worms, making them much easier for tree frogs to consume. Wax worms are very high in fat though, and should only be fed occasionally to prevent obesity and other health problems from developing. Store wax worms in the refrigerator to prolong their larval stage, or place them in a large, ventilated jar in a warm area of the house and allow them to pupate into moths to give your tree frog a flying treat.

Other Worms

Many other moth, fly, and beetle larvae have become available in recent years. Silkworms, tomato hornworms, butter worms, and phoenix worms are some that are often available from special feeder-insect companies. Silkworms in particular are a highly nutritious food item that can be fed regularly with good results, but they are relatively expensive when compared to other feeders.

True worms, such as earthworms or night crawlers, are another possible food item for tree frogs. Earthworms should be kept in soil and fed sliced vegetables or decaying leaves. Store them in a cool location, preferably between 40°F (4°C) and 60°F (16°C). Night crawlers are best kept cooler, ideally between 35°F (2°C) and 40°F (4°C). Large night crawlers are too big for most tree frogs to eat, so it may be helpful to cut them into smaller pieces. As long as it moves, tree frogs will recognize a chopped night crawler as food.

Cockroaches

A number of different cockroaches have recently gained popularity among frog keepers, and have proved to be easily cultured and nutritious. The bad stigma associated with roaches prevents many people from using them, but it's important to realize that, out of the thousands of cockroach species on this planet, only a few dozen are known to become pests within the household. By selecting a species of roach that cannot fly or climb glass, it's possible to contain and culture these creatures with little to no risk that they will escape and populate your house. Furthermore, the species commonly cultured for food are from tropical environments and require high humidity and warm temperatures to survive and reproduce; conditions that must be artificially created and are not present in most households.

The lobster roach (*Nauphoeta cinerea*), Turkistan roach (*Blatta lateralis*), discoid roach (*Blaberus discoidalis*), and Guyana orange-spotted roach (*Blaptica dubia*) are four common species that can make great feeders for tree frogs. The lobster roach and Turkistan roach are small, growing to around an inch (2.5 cm) in size as adults, while discoid and Guyana orange-spotted roaches grow large, sometimes up to 2 inches (5 cm). If a colony of roaches is set up, the juveniles can be used as food for smaller frogs, while adult roaches can be used to feed larger tree frog species. None of the four cockroaches mentioned above can fly, but it should be noted that lobster roaches are capable of climbing, so care should be taken to have a secure lid on their cage to prevent escapes.

Several species of roaches that are available commercially can be fed to tree frogs. These are Cuban green roaches.

A glass aquarium or plastic storage container with holes drilled in the cover can be used to store cockroaches. Most people choose to use a substrate of ground coconut husk fiber, sphagnum moss, or fir bark, although some have had success using no substrate at all. Cork bark or pieces of cardboard can be used as climbing areas and shelters. Warm temperatures are required to keep these cockroaches alive, so store them where temperatures stay between 78°F (26°C) and 95°F (35°C). A small reptile heat pad can be attached to the outside of the cage if heating is required.

Roaches are a nutritious food item, provided they are fed well. They are omnivores, and will consume just about anything—which makes feeding them easy. A healthy roach diet should consist of fresh fruits and vegetables, such as oranges, apples, sweet potatoes, yams, carrots, grapes, and romaine lettuce. Dry dog food or oats should be provided in addition to the fruits and vegetables. If too much food is offered at once, it often molds, so it's best to feed small quantities several times each week to prevent unsanitary conditions from developing. Remove old food at every feeding. Water can be provided with a moist sponge. It can also be helpful to lightly spray the cage with water once a week to maintain the required humidity level and keep the roaches hydrated.

How to Feed

If you haven't kept frogs before, you might be asking yourself the question "How the heck do I get crickets and roaches into the frog's cage?" There are many different techniques, and you likely will develop your own over time. Most use some sort of feeding container, such as a plastic cup, box, or bag. Crickets or roaches are shaken off their cardboard hiding spots into this container and then counted. Once an appropriate number has been gathered, pour a little supplement into the feeding container and shake the insects around in it until they are coated well. The feeders can then be taken to the tree frog cage and fed to the hungry amphibians inside.

Flightless Fruit Flies

Flightless fruit flies are a good occasional food for small species of tree frogs, and they are particularly useful for varying the diet of young frogs that have not grown to adult size. Two species of fruit fly are typically offered for sale, both are flightless. *Drosophila hydei* is a large species, reaching around 1/8 inch (0.3 cm). *Drosophila melanogaster* is about half the size of *Drosophila hydei*. Fruit flies are normally sold in cultures that consist of a container or vial with media on the bottom that the larvae feed on. A single culture can last for a month or more and produce thousands of flies over that period. Vials may be sold at some pet stores, but are best purchased from fruit-fly specialty stores on the Internet.

Houseflies

Houseflies are not as readily available as fruit flies, but are worth searching for because they offer an inexpensive, healthy food that can be used frequently to vary a tree frog's diet. Sometimes feeder insect companies offer flightless houseflies, but the normal flying variety is usually preferred because it allows tree frogs the opportunity to hunt flying prey. Houseflies are normally purchased in their larval stage. They can be found for sale on the Internet from biological supply companies, feeder-insect companies, and sometimes bait shops. The larvae should be left to sit at room temperature in a large, ventilated (but secure) container for a few days, during which time they will pupate into flying adults. Once most of the larvae have developed into flies, they can be stored in the refrigerator, where they will remain motionless because of the cool temperature. Immobile, refrigerated flies can then be shaken into a tree frog's cage, where they will slowly warm up and begin to fly again, providing an airborne meal that few tree frogs can resist.

Large tree frogs, like White's tree frogs, will eat small mice, but do not feed them to your frogs too often.

Mice

Some large species of tree frogs will gladly feed on newborn mice. Usually called pinky mice by pet stores due to their hairless pink skin, they should be used sparingly to add variety to a tree frog's diet. When fed frequently, nutritional problems may result, including obesity.

Wild Insects and Field Sweepings

Collecting your own insects from the wild is a good way to vary the tree frog diet. Grasshoppers, katydids, field crickets, grubs, mayflies, and moths are just a few types of insects that can easily be captured and fed to hungry tree frogs. It's important to only collect from areas that are free of pesticides, herbicides, or other chemicals that could harm amphibians. For this reason, avoid collecting near agricultural fields.

One of the best ways to collect wild insects and other invertebrates is to go field sweeping. In this method, a large mesh net is used to catch frog food. By walking through a field and continually running a fine net through tall grass, hundreds of insects can be collected. These are placed into a holding jar and offered to tree frogs just as other food would be. Rain or cool temperatures can ruin a day of field sweeping, so it's important to rely on other commercially available feeder insects as food, and to use wild insects to supplement a diet.

A word of caution: By offering wild insects to captive tree frogs it is likely that parasites will be introduced. Carefully weigh the pros and cons of feeding insects from the wild before venturing out into the field with a net. If you feed field sweepings, monitor the health of your frogs carefully for the presence of parasites.

Chapter 4

Breeding

Breeding tree frogs can be challenging because of the amount of time it requires, but the rewards are great. Frogs must be conditioned to breed, tadpoles must be cared for and, finally, large numbers of young tree frogs must be raised to a size large enough to sell. This process can take over half a year to complete, but is worth the effort.

More Than a Pair

Although it is possible to breed tree frogs with only a pair, often the best success is had with groups. Some have suggested that it's beneficial to have a male-heavy group for certain species because the competition between males can help stimulate breeding behavior.

Breeding tree frogs in captivity offers a rare chance to observe fascinating breeding behavior that few people have the privilege to witness. It also provides a way to reduce demand for wild-caught tree frogs by making captive-bred frogs available. Most tree frogs are not bred in captivity regularly so, for many species, breeding them can provide a fun challenge and may be an opportunity to do something few others have done in the past.

Sexing

Distinguishing between male and female tree frogs can be difficult. For every rule made to differentiate between sexes, an exception can be found in at least one species. For this reason, it's best to research the specific species of tree frog you are interested in breeding to determine how to tell males apart from females. Some of the best ways to sex tree frogs are outlined below.

In most species of frogs, the males call to attract mates. This is a male green tree frog calling.

Calling

A good method to sex many species is to listen for their call. Mature male tree frogs vocalize to attract mates, so if a frog calls it's often a male. Females of some species may also vocalize in response to the call of a male, making it difficult to distinguish males from females among these particular tree frogs. Both sexes will also emit distress calls when they are threatened, but this type of vocalization is not as pronounced as the loud advertisement call from a male. Frogs that have been calling for extended periods of time often have a dark or baggy-looking throat, so by examining it, you can often tell which frogs have been calling and which frogs have not.

Size

Adult female tree frogs are usually larger than males. In some species, females may be almost twice as large as males, while in others the size difference may be more subtle. In addition, females often have a slightly broader head or more robust appearance than males. Individual animals can vary a great deal in size and shape, with large males appearing to be females, and small or young females looking like males. The body structure and size of a tree frog are best used to sex them in addition to other more reliable methods.

Nuptial Pads

Nuptial pads are found on male tree frogs. They appear at the base of the thumb during breeding season, and are used to help grasp female frogs while in amplexus (the mating position). Usually, nuptial pads are dark in color and look rough in appearance when compared to the rest of the skin. They can be hard to see in some species, while in others they are fairly prominent. Nuptial pads only develop in male frogs during the breeding season or when males are conditioned to breed in captivity, but if they are present, the frog is unquestionably male.

The males of many tree frog species develop nuptial pads when in breeding condition, shown here on a waxy monkey frog.

Breeding

To breed tree frogs in captivity it's important to understand the basics of their breeding behavior. Breeding is initiated by loud advertisement calls produced by male frogs. The calls serve to attract females and, if a female is receptive, she will usually approach the male to signal she is ready to breed. Both will then move to a suitable place to spawn and the male will grasp the female from behind, holding on tightly with his forearms. This mating embrace is called amplexus.

Get a Group

Juvenile frogs will not call, have not reached their adult size, and will not develop nuptial pads, so they cannot be sexed. If breeding is the goal, and properly sexed adult frogs are unavailable, it is best to purchase a large group of juveniles at one time to increase the chances of getting a pair. Many tree frogs reach maturity in under a year, so if juveniles are purchased it will be possible to sex them soon enough.

As the female expels eggs, the male fertilizes them. Once complete, they then break from amplexus.

Most tree frogs breed during the wettest part of the year, when rain is frequent and water levels are high. To breed them in captivity, you must recreate these conditions by adjusting the temperature, humidity, and availability of water. Frogs from regions where there is little seasonal variation often breed year round as water is available, while those from environments that experience strong seasonal changes need a little more stimuli to reproduce in captivity. To encourage breeding, mist their cage frequently and/or construct a rain chamber to which the frogs can be moved to breed. For some species, it may even be helpful to flood the cage by pouring water on the substrate, saturating it until puddles form. Certain substrates, like soils, will spoil quickly when waterlogged, so change them when necessary if using this approach.

In addition to altering the temperature, humidity, and available water, it's also important to increase the availability of food. Feed often and use a variety of different foods. Females in particular must be fed well in order to breed, needing enough excess calories to produce hundreds and sometimes thousands of eggs.

It's important to carefully observe breeding groups to ensure that all frogs remain healthy, and that smaller or weaker animals are not bullied out of food by more aggressive ones. Additionally, breeding can be very stressful for frogs; this can weaken their immune system and make them more susceptible to diseases and other health problems. Only allow frogs that are in good health to breed because the stress from it may push weak or unhealthy individuals over the edge.

The Rain Chamber

Although some tree frogs can be bred in their usual cage, most breed best when moved to a separate one specifically designed for breeding purposes; this is called a rain chamber. A rain chamber can be made out of any waterproof container. The defining feature is a pump

Mexican leaf frogs in amplexus.

that circulates water from the bottom of the cage to the top, where it runs through a perforated tube or pipe called a rain bar. When the pump is turned on, water rains down from above, creating an artificial rainstorm.

Standard glass aquariums, acrylic cages, or plastic storage bins can all be used to make a rain chamber. In the bottom of the enclosure, place a submersible aquarium pump to move water from the bottom of the cage, up through the rain bar above. Attach PVC plastic pipe or flexible tubing to the output nozzle of the pump and direct it to the top of the cage, then horizontally across the top of the chamber. Perforate the horizontal section of pipe or flexible tubing with many small holes and cap off the end. If the pump is too powerful, streams of water will shoot out of the holes instead of individual drops. If this occurs, drill more holes to relieve some of the pressure or adjust the pump.

The bottom of the rain chamber can remain bare, without any gravel or stones. This will make water changes less trouble. A few inches of water must always be present in the bottom of the rain chamber for the pump to function. To prevent drowning of both frogs and feeder insects, scatter large rocks, pieces of driftwood, and floating sections of cork bark around the bottom of the tank. Some tree frogs will deposit their eggs on or around these items.

If strong lighting is provided, live plants can be grown in the water. Particularly useful are floating species like water lettuce (*Pistia stratiotes*), water hyacinth (*Eichhornia crassipes*), and Amazon frogbit (*Limnobium laevigatum*). Golden pothos (*Scindapsus aureus*) and peace lilies (*Spathiphyllum* species) can be grown with their leaves extending above the water's surface. Other plants can be grown in pots that are kept out of the water on top of platforms, like upside down flowerpots or plastic boxes. Ensure that all plants used are free of pesticides, herbicides, leaf polish, and other chemicals that could be harmful to amphibians. Using artificial plants may work equally well and can be a good alternative if you don't have a green thumb.

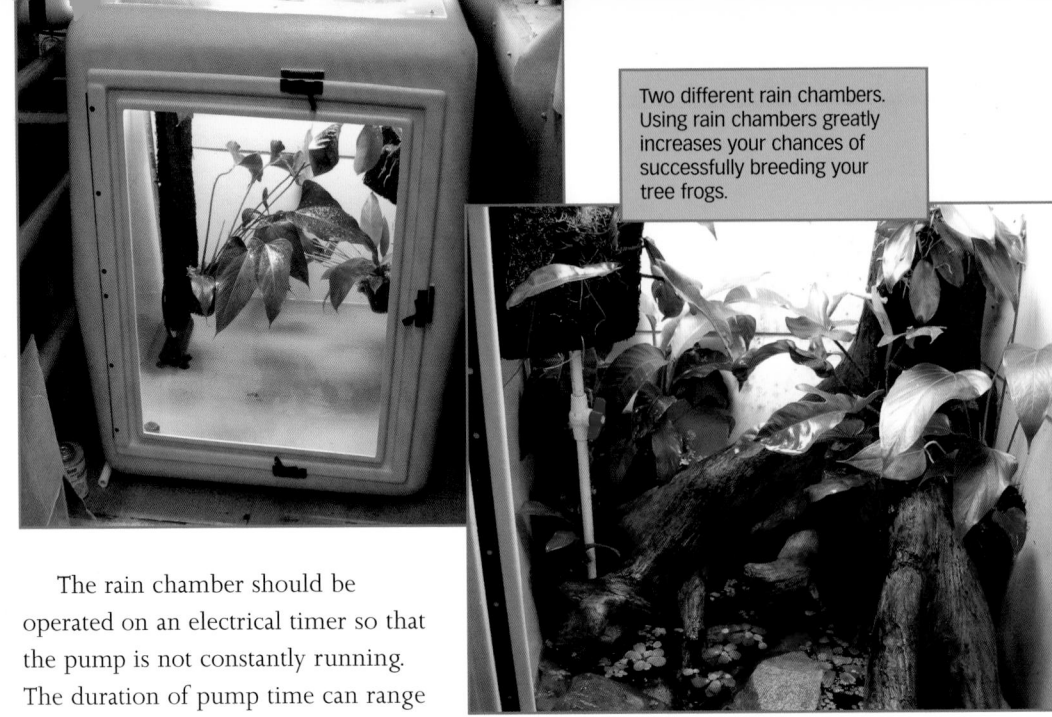

Two different rain chambers. Using rain chambers greatly increases your chances of successfully breeding your tree frogs.

The rain chamber should be operated on an electrical timer so that the pump is not constantly running. The duration of pump time can range from a few minutes to several hours, and it should be set to turn on during both the day and night. It's worth some experimentation to determine the frequency and length of time that best stimulates your frogs to breed.

Tree frogs may need to be moved back and forth from their permanent enclosure to the rain chamber if they do not successfully spawn the first time. Initially leaving the frogs in the rain chamber for 1 to 2 weeks, then moving them back to their original cage for that same amount of time, then back to the rain chamber following the break can yield good results.

Dry Period

Depending on the species you keep, you may need to put your tree frogs through a cool, dry period prior to the artificial wet season. This can help emphasize the difference between the seasons that are created and is needed to stimulate breeding behavior in certain species. During this dry period, the amount of ventilation should be increased, and the cage should no longer be misted. It can also be useful to decrease the temperature and reduce how much food is available. Ensure that all tree frogs exposed to these stressful conditions are in prime health, because weaker individuals may be unable to cope with them.

Know Your Frogs

Tree frogs utilize many different breeding strategies, so it's important to research the breeding habits of the particular species you are attempting to breed. Many tree frogs breed among emergent vegetation and require floating plants or other objects on which to deposit their eggs. Others breed above water on leaves that overhang small ponds or slow-moving streams. Some tree frogs have very clever breeding strategies and breed within trees, in water-filled holes and large cavities that have rotted away. Understanding the breeding habits of the species you are working with is important so that the specific conditions needed for breeding can be recreated.

Eggs

Tree frogs deposit their eggs several different ways. Many simply oviposit (lay eggs) on the water's surface. Others have evolved interesting ways of breeding out of water to avoid aquatic predators. A large number of tree frogs drape their eggs on floating or emergent vegetation. In captivity, floating water lettuce, duckweed, or plant clippings can be placed in a rain chamber to serve this purpose. The familiar red-eyed tree frog, along with many others, takes it a step further, and lays its eggs on leaves that overhang a body of water. As the tadpoles hatch, they wriggle free from the egg mass and drop into the water below.

Some tree frogs breed by creating what are called foam nests, producing a sticky mucus to coat the eggs once they are laid. While this is being expelled, they use their hind limbs to lather it into a giant, foamy, protective coating for the eggs that ensures they remain moist while developing.

Close-up view of the rain bar in one of the rain chambers.

Keep the Water Clean

It is very important that good water quality is maintained within the rain chamber, and that partial water changes are frequently preformed. If the water quality is neglected and harmful chemicals accumulate in it, the tree frogs will be harmed every time the pump is turned on and it rains!

Certain canopy-dwelling tree frogs do not use bodies of water on the ground in which to breed. Instead, they rely on water-filled cavities within trees to deposit their eggs and raise their tadpoles. The tree holes offer protection from predators and prevent the frogs from having to climb down to the ground to breed. In captivity, it's important to provide suitable conditions for the particular species you are breeding to deposit eggs, whether it is an artificial tree hole, plants overhanging water, or a layer of floating vegetation.

If spawning is successful and eggs are fertile, they will visibly start to develop within days of being laid. The ovum of fertile eggs looks like it is splitting down the center, and it will soon start to take the form of a tadpole. Infertile eggs quickly mold and begin to decay, often being discolored. It's fairly common for only part of a clutch to be fertile. In this situation, it may be necessary to use a moist paper towel or razor blade to carefully remove infertile eggs from those that are fertile and developing. This prevents the mold and unwanted bacteria that grow on the infertile eggs from spreading onto fertile ones.

Eggs should remain moist and be kept in a humid container to ensure that they do not dry out. If laid in a rain chamber, they can be left to develop and hatch into the water below. Eggs laid in the permanent cage should be removed and placed in a different enclosure. For species that deposit eggs around objects

Most tree frogs come down from the trees to lay eggs in the water, as this pair of White's tree frogs is doing.

Most species of tree frogs lay dozens or hundreds of eggs. These are Mexican leaf frog eggs.

near the surface of the water, it is easiest to simply leave the eggs in the cage and then move the tadpoles once they hatch. Eggs that are laid on plant leaves should be moved before the tadpoles break free by removing the entire leaf. Suspend the egg-covered leaf above shallow water in a small container, such as a deli cup or jar. Limit or completely restrict the ventilation in this container to prevent desiccation of the eggs.

Initial Tadpole Care

Tadpoles break free from their eggs a few days to a couple weeks after being laid, depending on the species and the conditions to which the eggs are exposed. Initially, tadpoles may appear motionless or dead as they lay on the bottom of the aquarium, living off the remaining nutrients from their yolk sack. At this stage, it is best to keep the tadpoles in very shallow water, with little to no water current. As they develop, they begin to move more frequently, scavenging for food and moving about their new aquatic world. Once they are mobile, the water level can be increased and any pumps or filters turned on.

Housing Tadpoles

The container in which tadpoles are kept can range in size from a small plastic box, to a standard 20-gallon (75.7-l) aquarium, to a child's small swimming pool. Use the largest volume of water possible, because the greater the volume of water used, the less concentrated waste will be. Larger volumes of water also provide more stable conditions because they are less likely to experience swings in temperature or water quality.

Above the container, fluorescent lights should be suspended to encourage algae growth, which many tadpoles feed on. The light also provides a way to grow live plants. Aquatic, floating, and emergent plant species can all be used. As the plants grow, they use up excess nutrients and nitrates in the water, which helps maintain good water quality. Other than live plants, the container can remain fairly bare. I prefer to use a bare bottom when raising tadpoles, avoiding substrates like gravel or river rocks. This makes it easier to do water

Be Prepared

Some tree frogs can lay thousands of eggs. It can take large amounts of time and space to care for all the resulting tadpoles and frogs, so plan carefully before tossing a pair of frogs into a rain chamber.

changes and siphon detritus from the bottom. Some breeders submerge dried leaves into their tadpole tanks. Most often oak, magnolia, or Indian almond leaves are used. These release beneficial tannins into the water and offer hiding spots for the tadpoles. The bio-film that grows on leaves as they decay can also provide food for many species.

Water Quality

Maintaining good water quality is essential to successfully raising tadpoles. Partial water changes should be performed at least once a week, and sometimes as often as every other day if the tadpoles are stocked heavily. Use a siphon or turkey baster to suck up the waste that accumulates on the bottom. Ensure that the water used to fill the tank back up is the same temperature as the water already in the tank to prevent temperature shocks. Also, avoid changing more than half the water at one time, so that no large fluctuations in water quality occur, and to prevent the removal of too many beneficial bacteria. These microscopic organisms help break down waste and maintain stable conditions; if too many are removed during a water change, water quality problems result. You may wish to set up tadpole tanks well in advance of breeding your frogs, even keeping a few fish in them while tadpoles are absent. This will guarantee that the tanks are ready for tadpoles when your frogs breed.

Choose the source of water used for the tadpoles carefully. Tap water that has been treated with a conditioner and is free of chlorine, chloramines, and heavy metals may be suitable. The quality of tap water varies among different locations and, in some areas, it may not be safe for tadpoles. Tap water that is very hard or has been found to have nitrates or other harmful chemicals in it should not be used. Bottled spring water can be used as an alternative in this situation. Avoid using pure distilled or reverse-osmosis water because these do not contain essential trace elements and salts that may be important for tadpole development. In areas with hard water, start with distilled or reverse-osmosis water, then add some conditioned tap water. This will add the needed salts and minerals to the pure water, and the result will be diluted tap water that is safe for tadpoles.

Filtration

Filtration can be used to help maintain water quality but is not necessary in every situation. The most common type of filter used with tadpoles is the sponge filter. These are powered by an air pump and work well for filtering small volumes of water. Power filters that hang over the side of a tank can be used instead, and are very effective. Canister filters are another type of filtration that can work well, but are best for filtering large-volume, heavily stocked tanks. The intake tubes of both power filters and canister filters must be covered with a pre-filter to prevent tadpoles from being sucked into them. Many tadpoles develop in fairly stagnant water in the wild so it's often best to set these filters on their lowest setting to prevent too much water movement. The outputs of the filters can be deflected as well, to reduce flow. Undergravel filters are not practical when temporarily raising tadpoles, so avoid using them. If a small number of tadpoles is being raised, a filter isn't even necessary, provided that frequent water changes are preformed.

Nitrifying Bacteria

Fortunately, you are not the only one responsible for the water quality in a tadpole aquarium—helpful bacteria are also at work. They convert the dangerous ammonium and nitrite produced by decomposing waste into the less harmful chemical nitrate. Nitrate is what you are in charge of removing from the aquarium, thus maintaining tadpole-friendly water conditions in a team effort with nitrifying bacteria.

Feeding Tadpoles

Most tadpoles are herbivores and initially feed on different types of algae. Many will also scavenge on detritus and bacteria. As their mouths develop, some tadpoles will start to consume plant leaves and aquatic vegetation. Many different diets are available to feed captive tadpoles. High quality fish food is often the easiest to offer, and it works well for many species. Multiple types of fish food can be used, from standard tropical community flake to sinking algae wafers. Some tadpoles will appreciate the addition of thawed bloodworms or daphnia every few feedings. Using different types of food to vary a tadpole's diet can help prevent nutritional deficiencies from developing. In addition to fish food, diets specifically designed for tadpoles work well. These are available from biological supply companies as well as many pet stores. Other foods used to vary a tadpole's diet include crushed aquatic turtle pellets, powdered algae supplements (such as spirulina or chlorella, available from health food stores), and unflavored nori.

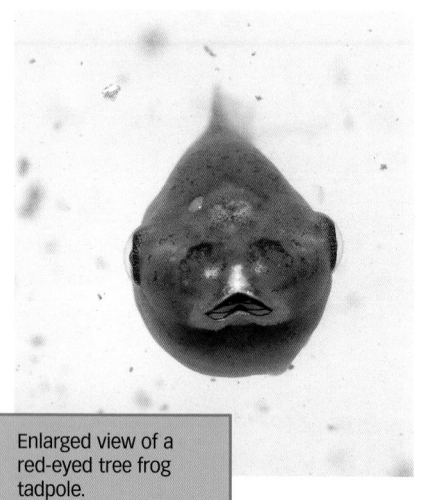

Enlarged view of a red-eyed tree frog tadpole.

Tadpoles should be fed daily, as much as they will consume without spoiling the water. If food is left over after several hours, it's a good sign that too much is being fed. It's advantageous to feed in small amounts several times each day if possible, although tadpoles are generally hardy and will live fine if not fed for a few days, scavenging on algae and detritus growing in the tank when prepared foods are unavailable.

Metamorphosis

The transitional period between the aquatic larval stage of a tree frog and the terrestrial adult form is a time in which tree frogs require special care. Once front arms develop, the tail begins to be absorbed, and the tiny tailed tree frogs need a way to easily access land so that they don't drown. It can take anywhere from a few weeks to a few months for tadpoles to reach this point.

Once front arms develop, many tadpole species will climb up the side of the container they are being raised in. At this stage, they can be caught and moved to a different cage, where they will finish absorbing their tail without the risk of drowning. Other tree frogs need an easier way to access land. Sometimes, floating a few pieces of cork bark in the water can provide enough solid area for developing tree frogs. Plants will also be used by newly morphed frogs as a surface on which to emerge. Position clippings of pothos so that their leaves extend out of the water to provide a place for freshly metamorphosed tree frogs to climb onto. Floating water lettuce can also be used. Once tadpoles start to leave the water, it's important to secure a tight-fitting screen cover over the aquarium to prevent escapes.

Caring for Young Frogs

The first few weeks after leaving the water, tree frogs are very delicate. Keep young tree frogs in small, simple enclosures. A standard 10-gallon (38 l) aquarium lined with a moist paper towel substrate, a potted plant, and a shallow water dish works very well for most species. This setup may be able to initially house as many as 15 or 20 newly morphed tree frogs. It often becomes apparent after a few weeks that certain individuals within the group are growing faster than the rest. Separate growing tree frogs by size, housing all the larger ones together and the smaller ones in another cage. This helps ensure that no frogs get out-competed for food by stronger individuals.

Young tree frogs are particularly susceptible to desiccation, so a bowl of clean water must always be made available. This should be changed at least once a day. Drowning can be a risk for some newly morphed tree frogs, especially in large, smooth-sided water bowls. To prevent drowning, submerge a paper towel in the water dish to give the small frogs some footing and an easy way out. The paper towel should be changed everyday, along with the water.

Feeding them is the most challenging part of raising large numbers of young tree frogs. At first, freshly morphed tree frogs will live off the nutrients provided by their absorbed tail, but a few days after the tail is fully absorbed they will need to be fed every night.

Don't Overfeed

It's easy to overfeed tadpoles and spoil their water. Pay close attention to how fast tadpoles consume their food, and make sure to siphon out uneaten leftovers.

Hundreds of frogs can be produced from a small group of breeding adults and, with each young tree frog eating anywhere from two to ten or more food items every evening, thousands of crickets, fruit flies, or other feeder insects may be required each week. It's usually necessary to start ordering crickets and other feeders in bulk from reptile food distributors. Lightly dust food items in vitamin or calcium supplements at nearly every feeding while the young frogs are growing to ensure nutritional requirements are met.

Once the tree frogs reach a large enough size, they can be sold, traded, or given away. Allow a minimum of 1 month to go by before selling tree frogs so that you are sure that all are healthy and ready for new homes.

When your tadpoles develop legs, you must provide them with a way to leave the water. A orange-legged monkey froglet is shown here.

Chapter 5

Health Care

Many different health problems can affect captive tree frogs. Internal parasites, bacterial infections, obesity, nutritional deficiencies, and abrasions are some of the common ones. Having a general understanding of how these and other problems develop, and what treatment involves, will help you both avoid them and keep you prepared in case they show up.

Most often, the poor health of tree frogs is directly related to the environment in which they're kept. Keeping the cage clean is one of the easiest ways to avoid sickness and disease. Changing the water dish daily is also important. Temperature plays a role in the health of tree frogs as well. Monitor the temperature closely, and ensure that it stays within the appropriate range, avoiding stressful fluctuations. By providing a clean cage and maintaining a suitable temperature range, many common health issues can be avoided.

Veterinarians

Locating a veterinarian who is experienced with amphibians can be difficult. Frogs don't need to be brought to the vet for yearly checkups like a dog or a cat, but they should be examined at the first sign of something wrong. If you aren't able to find a vet who is frog savvy in your area, your local "furry-creature" vet will still be able help by consulting other veterinarians elsewhere.

Stress

Stress weakens the immune system and makes tree frogs more susceptible to disease, so a simple way to prevent your frog from getting sick is to keep stressful situations to a minimum. Many factors heighten stress levels. Handling, overfeeding, breeding, being housed in inappropriate conditions or with too many other frogs, and being moved to a new cage are some common causes of stress. Keep interactions with tree frogs to a minimum, and ensure that their surroundings meet their needs in order to keep their immune system up to par.

Poisoning

Tree frogs have delicate, permeable skin that makes them very susceptible to contaminates. When cleaning their cage, avoid using soaps or other cleaners; if a residue is left behind, it could be dangerous to the frogs. Certain air deodorizers and sprays can also contaminate tree frog cages, so do not use these in the same room a frog is kept in. Our hands are another potential source of harmful chemicals, so always give them a quick rinse with water before handling tree frogs or touching things inside the cage. In addition, frogs can be poisoned from the

Keepers should quarantine wild-caught frogs, like this red-eyed, because they frequently have parasites or bacterial infections.

waste they excrete. When this builds up in a concentrated source, such as a water bowl that has not been changed for a while, tree frogs can essentially poison themselves.

Obesity

Most pet tree frogs are obese. This is understandable; we love to feed our frogs. Watching them eat is one of the most enjoyable parts of keeping them, but feeding too frequently or in too large amounts can easily lead to obesity. In addition, the cages that tree frogs are kept in are only a small fraction of the size of the environment they inhabit naturally, so they have far less room to move around, hunt, and use up the calories they consume. Obese tree frogs will have folds of skin and fat on their body, often over their eyes or under their chin. Fat deposits can cause major problems for amphibians, just as they can for humans, so it is best to put obese tree frogs on a diet. To do this, reduce both the quantity and frequency with which they are fed, and avoid foods that are high in fat, such as wax worms or super worms. The best plan is to avoid obesity in the first place by carefully paying attention to how much food you offer.

Finding a Herp Vet

It is not always easy to find vets who are experienced with reptiles and amphibians. Here are some suggestions to help you locate a vet who can help with your pet tree frogs. It is best if you locate one before you actually have an emergency.

- Call veterinarians listed as "exotic" or "reptile" vets in the phone book. Ask them if they are familiar with frogs, especially tree frogs.
- Ask at your local pet stores, herpetological society, animal shelters, and zoos to see if they can recommend someone.
- Contact the Association of Reptilian and Amphibian Veterinarians. Their web site is www.arav.org.

Metabolic Bone Disease

One of the most common problems related to diet is metabolic bone disease (MBD). This term is used to describe a variety of conditions resulting from a lack of calcium and/or vitamin D_3, or an imbalance between those and phosphorus. Tree frogs affected with MBD have skeletal deformities and fractures, and may look misshapen, particularly around the mouth or limbs. Lethargic behavior, tremors, and difficulty moving due to bone fractures often accompany the deformed appearance of tree frogs suffering from this disease.

Bloating versus Obesity

Sometimes tree frogs swell with a fluid or gas and become bloated. Bloating can be caused by bacterial infections, constipation, and kidney damage, among other things. Do not confuse bloating with obesity. They can easily be told apart because obese tree frogs have wrinkles and folds of skin around their head and body, while bloated frogs look expanded, as if their body has been pumped full of air. Bloated tree frogs should be examined by a veterinarian as soon as possible to determine what is causing the problem.

MBD can be avoided by feeding tree frogs a well-balanced diet that contains proper levels of calcium, vitamin D_3, and phosphorus. Phosphorus inhibits calcium intake and, because most feeder insects available are already high in phosphorus and low in calcium, use a phosphorus-free calcium supplement. In addition, the supplement must contain vitamin D_3, which allows tree frogs to properly use the calcium from their diet. Young, growing tree frogs should have their food supplemented with calcium more often than adults that have already matured. If any sign of MBD is noticed, contact a veterinarian. He will be able to properly diagnose the problem, and will likely provide additional forms of calcium supplementation for your tree frog.

Impaction

A tree frog is an excellent predator, but sometimes, along with the food it catches also comes some of the substrate it is being kept on. This can become lodged and block its digestive tract. Avoid impaction by using a substrate that is either so fine it is unlikely to cause an impaction (coconut husk fiber, certain soils, etc.), or one that cannot easily be ingested (paper towels, foam rubber, large river stones, etc.). Symptoms of impaction include a slightly bloated abdomen and lethargic behavior. Surgery is generally required to help amphibians whose digestive tract is clogged.

White's tree frog is a species that is especially prone towards obesity when kept as a pet.

Bacterial Infections

Tree frogs, and all organisms for that matter, are constantly surrounded by bacteria. Normally, this doesn't present a problem for a healthy captive frog whose immune system is in good shape, but when the frog is weakened by improper care, a bacterial infection may start to develop. It can be difficult to diagnose these infections before they have progressed too far, so the best course of action is to prevent conditions that are favorable for bacterial infections. This includes keeping the enclosure clean and changing the water frequently, but also keeping stressful conditions to a minimum. Symptoms of bacterial infections include lethargy, bloating, skin discoloration, clouded eyes, paralysis, and/or twitching. Antibiotics can be used successfully to treat bacterial infections, and these can be acquired from a veterinarian.

Lifespan

Even when provided with the best care, captive tree frogs will not live forever. Most species should live for at least 5 to 10 years in captivity, and some, such as White's tree frog (*Litoria caerulea*), have been recorded as living for over 20 years.

Fungal Infections

Fungal infections are less common than bacterial infections in tree frogs. Localized infections occasionally show up on wounds or open sores. They often appear as a slimy gray or otherwise discolored ring surrounding the wound, or they may cover the entire area, forming an unusually light-colored spot or blotch. Fungal infections can take many other forms though, and may appear differently depending on the type. For this reason, it's important to have a veterinarian inspect and then diagnose any suspected fungal infections so that the frog can be medicated appropriately.

More common than fungal infections affecting adult frogs are those that infect their tadpoles. During this aquatic stage of life, tree frogs are more susceptible to fungal infections. White fuzz is a clear sign of a fungal infection, so if you notice any on a tadpole, consider testing the water quality. Fish antifungal medications sold at pet stores can sometimes be used to successfully treat tadpoles with fungal infections.

Chytrid

One fungal infection in particular has caused much concern in recent years. *Batrachochytrium dendrobatidis* has been identified as a fungus responsible for many of the recently noticed amphibian population declines and extinctions. This fungus also shows up in captive

Red-Leg Disease

The infamous red-leg disease is a bacterial infection often caused by *Aeromonas* species. The name of this illness comes from the reddening of the skin, often on the underside of the legs, caused by broken capillaries that result from infection. The red legs are usually accompanied by other symptoms of a bacterial infection. Unfortunately, symptoms don't often appear until the frog has progressed too far to be treated. *Aeromonas* are common within soil and water and may be present in tree frog tanks without causing problems. Frogs with a weakened immune system are likely to develop the infection, so by keeping stress to a minimum and your tree frog's immune system strong, you can avoid red-leg disease.

amphibians occasionally, and it is capable of killing frogs within weeks of infection. Conversely, evidence also suggests that some frogs can live with this fungal infection for years without showing symptoms, infecting others and their environment as they live contentedly, appearing normal to their keeper. Drops in temperature and stress have been suggested as the cause of *Batrachochytrium dendrobatidis* outbreaks in captive amphibians. Often called chytrid for short, this fungal infection can be treated successfully, but it must be properly diagnosed by a veterinarian so that the appropriate medication can be provided. Symptoms include lethargy, lack of appetite, frequently shedding skin, and soaking in water for prolonged periods of time, sometimes constantly.

Parasites

An assortment of microscopic critters infest the insides of most tree frogs. They can inhabit the gut, lungs, muscles, skin, and even blood, using the frogs as a host. The negative image most people have of parasites cause many to become alarmed at hearing their frog may be filled with them but, much of the time, parasites aren't worth worrying about. Captive frogs can live long lives with parasite infections, provided the parasites don't reach elevated levels. A weakened immune system caused by stress or another health problem can allow parasite populations to grow too large for tree frogs to cope with—then parasites become problematic for their hosts. Bring a fecal sample to your veterinarian to allow him to determine what types of parasites are present in your frog and what treatment will be suitable. Consider bringing fecal samples of newly acquired frogs to your vet to initially see if they need to be treated. After that, have feces examined when frogs appear lethargic, malnourished, or otherwise unhealthy.

Abrasions, Wounds, and Trauma

Minor scrapes and abrasions are fairly common problems. Often kept in small enclosures while being temporarily housed and transported by dealers or retailers, many tree frogs damage themselves by jumping into the side of the cage or continually rubbing their face against it. Small wounds sometimes heal without treatment, but if the abrasion is not healing after a couple of days, contact a veterinarian.

Saline solutions are recommended as treatment and can be applied using a cotton swab, rinsing the wound again with fresh water after a few minutes. Antibiotic ointments are also frequently used to treat wounds and resulting infections. More serious injuries can be the result of a tree frog being wounded by a sharp object in the cage, or a mistake made by the keeper, such as dropping a heavy cage item on a frog. Contact a veterinarian as soon as possible if serious trauma occurs.

Quarantine Quickly

The first step to take when you notice a health problem is to quarantine the affected frog away from others in the cage. Set it up in a simple cage that is easy to clean and allows you to monitor its condition closely.

Rectal Proplapses

A prolapse occurs when an internal organ slips out of place. Rectal prolapses are most often noticed in tree frogs, when internal tissue hangs out of the vent. This can be very alarming when first noticed, appearing as though your tree frog is defecating part of its insides. The causes of a rectal prolapse are usually related to diet, and can be the result of impaction, MBD, or gastric overload, in which the frog has simply been fed too much. Intestinal parasites and poisoning are also suspected causes of rectal prolapses. Sometimes the muscle or tissue that has fallen out of place will simply fix itself, but other times a prolapse requires the assistance of a veterinarian. Dabbing the protruding tissue with sugar water will reduce swelling and often aid the situation. If the exposed tissue does not retreat after 24 hours, contact a veterinarian immediately.

Wild-caught tree frog often suffer from rostral abrasions, shown here on barking tree frogs.

Chapter 6

The Green Tree Frog and Other North American *Hyla* Species

The green tree frog (*Hyla cinerea*) was my first pet amphibian and is so for many people. These inexpensive little tree frogs are one of the most common pet frogs. A few other *Hyla* species from North America also find their way into the pet trade with some frequency, including the squirrel tree frog (*H. squirella*), barking tree frog (*H. gratiosa*), Cope's gray tree frog (*H. chrysoscelis*), and eastern gray tree frog (*H. versicolor*), among others. These North American natives can make exceptional captives when they are provided with the proper care, and they are a good choice for both novice and expert keepers alike. This chapter focuses on the care of North American *Hyla* species, using the care of the green tree frog as model for the rest.

Description of Species
Green Tree Frog

The green tree frog (H. cinerea) is native to the southeastern United States. It is common around areas of water such as swamps, marshes, slow-moving streams, lakesides, and even cattle watering troughs. The leaves of emergent vegetation (plants that are rooted underwater, but grow above the water surface) serve as favorite perches and resting spots during the day.

As adults, green tree frogs measure slightly over 2.0 inches (5.1 cm) in length, although many individuals stay smaller. They are predominantly bright green in color but are capable of changing to a darker brown or olive green depending on the environmental conditions to which they are exposed. Most have a cream or yellow lateral stripe that runs from their mouth down their flanks, but this may be absent from frogs of certain populations. An albino variety of green tree frog is also occasionally available, having ghostly white, almost translucent skin and pink eyes.

Green tree frogs are common frogs, both in nature and in the pet trade.

Squirrel Tree Frog

Very similar in appearance to the green tree frog, the squirrel tree frog (H. squirella) is slightly smaller, ranging in size from just under 1.0 inch (2.5 cm) to 1.5 inches (3.8 cm). Squirrel tree frogs lack the distinct lateral stripe of the green tree frog, although in certain individuals a line can still vaguely be seen running down their side. In addition, some squirrel tree frogs may have dark, blotchy patterns on their backs. They inhabit environments similar to those of the green tree frog but have a slightly smaller distribution across the southeastern United States. In captivity, their care is identical to that of the green tree frog.

Barking Tree Frog

The barking tree frog (H. gratiosa) is also native to the southeastern United States. In the wild, this species spends much of its time high in trees, and it occupies wooded areas near water. During dry or hot parts of the year, barking tree frogs often climb down to the ground and burrow in the soil, where they aestivate until conditions improve.

They are the largest native tree frog in the United States, with

Squirrel tree frogs are very similar to green tree frogs, but they are smaller and lack the white lateral stripe.

some individuals growing to over 2.5 inches (6.4 cm) in length. Barking tree frogs are attractively patterned, usually with small, dark spots covering their dorsal sides. They are able to change colors from lime green to dark brown, usually appearing somewhere in between. Barking tree frogs can be somewhat more sensitive in captivity than the other species discussed in this chapter, but are by no means difficult to keep. They should be provided with a roomy, well-ventilated terrarium, larger than that used to house green tree frogs, but otherwise similar.

Gray Tree Frogs

Two gray tree frogs also find their way into the pet trade with some regularity. Cope's gray tree frog (*H. chrysoscelis*) and the eastern gray tree frog (*H. versicolor*) look identical. They have textured skin, covered in tiny bumps or warts. Adult frogs can change color, varying from bright white, to shades of gray, and even green. On the inner sides of their thighs are bright yellow or orange markings. Gray tree frogs mature to a size between 1.3 and 2.3 inches (3.3 and 5.8 cm). The two species range across most of the eastern US and southern Canada, from Oklahoma and southern Manitoba east to the coast.

These frogs are masters of disguise and can blend in exceptionally well with the bark of trees—surfaces on which they often rest during the day. They inhabit wooded areas, but are sometimes found in suburban developments, provided there are plenty of trees and a source of water available. Gray tree frogs make excellent pets and tolerate a large range of conditions.

Careful with Cooling

Only expose healthy frogs that have been in your care for an extended period to the somewhat harsh conditions of a cool, artificial winter. This goes for green tree frogs or any other species.

Some have suggested they may need to be put through a dormant period in the winter to survive in captivity, but I have not found this to be true.

Captive Care

Green tree frogs are hardy captives when purchased in good condition. They do not have very difficult or complex care requirements and, provided they are given the proper care, can live many years in captivity.

Male barking tree frog calling on the surface of a pond. The call of this species is a loud, dog-like bark, hence the common name.

Acquisition

The majority of green tree frogs offered for sale are unfortunately wild-caught. They are captured by a collector, sent to a dealer, and then shipped to a pet store. While in the care of a collector or dealer, green tree frogs are often heavily stocked in small enclosures, which can be very stressful. Do not purchase any green tree frog if others in the cage look unhealthy or sick, and obviously pass up any sick-looking individuals.

An alternative to buying the heavily stocked, sometimes unhealthy, wild-caught green tree frogs is to catch one yourself. If you live within their range and it is legal, consider spending a night outside by the pond looking for a green tree frog. You will likely end up with a healthy animal, and will not be encouraging the large-scale commercial collecting that supplies the pet trade.

Housing

Green tree frogs are simple to house. They are tolerant of many different styles of housing and tend to do equally well in both simple, hygienic enclosures and more natural setups. Heating sometimes isn't even required, thus simplifying their enclosure further. I recommend keeping them in a very simple setup initially so that they can be monitored carefully to ensure they are healthy. Then switch them to a more natural habitat down the line if desired.

Although they are small tree frogs, they should not be kept in small enclosures. Green tree frogs are very active and will use all the room they are provided with. A pair can successfully be kept in a standard 10-gallon (38 l) aquarium or other enclosure of similar size. Use a secure screen cover to allow plenty of ventilation.

Inside the cage a substrate, water bowl, perches, and hide spots are needed. A simple enclosure can consist of an aquarium lined with moist paper towels or upholstery foam rubber. Paper towels should be changed several times a week, but these are cheap and hygienic.

If you want a more natural appearance, opt for ground coconut husk fiber. A potted plant or two can be placed in a section of the cage to offer cover as well as something for the frogs to climb on. Artificial plants can be used if you don't have luck with live ones.

The two species of gray tree frog are identical in appearance; they have different calls and genetics.

Driftwood or cork bark slabs make excellent perches, although much of the time I find green tree frogs prefer to simply rest on the side of the tank during the day. A large but shallow water dish should also be provided. This must be changed daily to prevent the buildup of waste.

Temperature and Humidity

Green tree frogs are tolerant of a wide range of temperatures. Generally, a daytime temperature between 72°F (22°C) and 80°F (27°C) works well, with occasional days outside of this range not presenting a problem. The temperature at night can drop by 5°F to 10°F (3°C–6°C). Sometimes heating will be necessary during cooler times of the year. A 15- to 50-watt heat lamp is usually sufficient, depending on the size of the enclosure.

The humidity level in the cage can vary quite a bit without problems. In the wild, after heavy rains, green tree frogs may experience humidity levels near 100 percent, while during the cool, sometimes dry winters, humidity can fall drastically. In captivity, mist their cage a few times a week to maintain moderate humidity levels. If the cage is in a particularly dry room, it may be necessary to mist the cage more often so that it does not completely dry out.

Diet

Like most frogs in captivity, green tree frogs must be provided with live insects for food. Crickets can make up the majority of their diet. Offer anywhere from two to six crickets every second or third day, depending on the size of the crickets and the size of the frog. They will enthusiastically hunt flying insects, such as moths or houseflies so, when possible, use these to vary their diet. Earthworms can also be offered, and are particularly useful for feeding the larger, closely related gray and barking tree frogs.

Green tree frogs often turn brown in color when they are resting or feeling cold.

Breeding

Few herp hobbyists breed green tree frogs in captivity with any consistency. This is not necessarily because they are difficult to breed, but because they are cheap and easily collected from the wild. This should not deter anyone from attempting to breed these frogs. It would be very nice to see healthy, captive-bred stock available to replace the commonly unhealthy, wild-caught green tree frogs most often found for sale.

Sexing The most reliable way to distinguish male green tree frogs from females is to listen for their call, which sounds something like a high-pitched duck quack. Only male green tree frogs vocalize, and they do so in captivity frequently after having their cage misted. If you can't figure out which frog is calling, examine their throats the following morning. Males often have a darkened or somewhat baggy-looking throat after spending extended periods of time vocalizing. Like many tree frogs, it's best to have multiple males in a breeding group because it's thought the competition between them may help stimulate breeding behavior.

Conditioning Seasonal cycling and proper conditioning are usually necessary to evoke a breeding response. The goal is to replicate those seasonal changes green tree frogs experience in the wild that stimulate them to breed. This means cooling their cage by 10°F or even 15°F degrees (6°C–8°C) for several weeks to simulate winter. During this period, allow the substrate to dry and the humidity level to decrease. Food should also be limited during this period. A clean source of water must always remain available to ensure the frogs stay hydrated during this sometimes stressful artificial winter.

Following this dry, cool season, the frogs must be convinced that it's spring—the start of the breeding season. First, begin offering food more readily and in somewhat larger amounts. The females must eat well to produce eggs. Also, increase the temperature as well as the humidity by frequently spraying the cage several times a day.

At this point, the males should begin to call loudly at night if they have been conditioned properly. Once the females have swelled with eggs and the males are calling, the group can be moved to a rain chamber, where breeding will take place. Female green tree frogs produce hundreds of eggs. They are laid most often on floating vegetation, such as duckweed.

Greens in the Terrarium

Green tree frogs are great candidates for a living terrarium. Because of their small size, they rarely damage plants as other larger species would, and they are not overly messy, so the waste they produce won't overload a well-maintained, established terrarium.

Blue green tree frogs—lacking yellow pigments—are bred in small numbers for the pet trade.

Tadpole and Froglet Care Hundreds or even thousands of tadpoles can be produced from a single breeding period in the rain chamber. These should be cared for as described in the breeding chapter. Large aquariums, plastic storage containers, or small plastic swimming pools may be required to house the large numbers of tadpoles, which will usually metamorphose into tiny green tree frogs within 5 to 8 weeks. These newly morphed frogs must be fed heavily, and will grow well on a diet of mostly crickets and occasional flightless fruit flies. It is best to keep them in simply furnished enclosures to make maintaining their environment easy.

Chapter 7

Red-eyed Tree Frog

Of all the tree frogs discussed in this book, perhaps the most familiar is the red-eyed tree frog (*Agalychnis callidryas*). They make wonderful captives, although are somewhat more sensitive than other commonly available species. This should not discourage you from keeping them though. As long as certain requirements are met, and healthy frogs are acquired to begin with, red-eyed tree frogs make excellent pet frogs.

Red-eyed tree frogs have beautiful blue markings on their sides that vary in brightness over the species range.

Description

With their green dorsum and limbs, red-eyed tree frogs blend in exceptionally well with the leaves under which they rest during the day. At night, this green coloration usually darkens, sometimes to a brownish purple, and it will also vary during the day depending on environmental factors, such as light intensity. Sometimes white spots are also present on the dorsum of certain individuals. The flanks are attractively patterned in stripes of blue and yellow, and their enlarged feet are bright orange. Adding to their colorful appearance, they have large, bright red eyes.

The coloration of red-eyed tree frogs can vary somewhat between populations. In general, those from northern parts of their range look like the red-eyed tree frog most are familiar with, having tomato red eyes and dark blue sides, distinctly striped in yellow. Those from southern populations often have darker, even burgundy eyes, and display lighter blue on the sides of their bodies. As adults, the larger female red-eyed tree frogs can reach nearly 3.0 inches (7.6 cm), while males generally stay smaller, usually around 2.0 inches (5.1 cm).

In the pet trade, quite a few different morphs or color varieties of red-eyed tree frogs are available. The most well-known is the xanthic form, which is predominantly pale yellow, with the exception of the sides of the body, which are striped in light purple. Their eyes also are no longer red, but white. A newly available albino red-eyed tree frog also exists. It is a brighter yellow than the xanthic form, and it retains the red eyes of normal red-eyed tree frogs. In addition, a very unusual black morph of the red-eyed tree frog has also recently become available. These frogs are solid black, with the exception of their ventral side, which is the normal pinkish off-white. A rare axanthic color form that is blue instead of green also exists, but is rarely available.

Natural History

Red-eyed tree frogs live throughout Central America, with their range starting at the southern end of Mexico and extending down through Panama. Some populations are even reported in northern Columbia. They inhabit tropical forests near temporary or permanent

bodies of water. During the day, red-eyed tree frogs rest on leaves and other surfaces, camouflaging themselves by concealing their bright colors. Red-eyed tree frogs (and other members of the subfamily Phyllomedusinae) are also often called red-eyed leaf frogs because of their preference for sleeping on the underside of leaves. It's been suggested that the vivid stripes on their sides, orange feet, and bright red eyes startle predators as the patterns and colors are exposed if a frog is disturbed.

Care in Captivity

The basic care of red-eyed tree frogs is uncomplicated, but the keeper must meet certain requirements in order for them to do well. They are less forgiving of inappropriate conditions than are other common pet tree frogs and, for this reason, it's important to research their care well before purchasing them to ensure you can meet their needs.

Red-eyed tree frogs often sleep on the undersides of leaves, where their green coloration conceals them.

Acquisition

Both captive-bred and wild-caught red-eyed tree frogs are available through pet stores, dealers, and breeders. Purchase red-eyed tree frogs that were produced in captivity whenever possible. Although often small and fragile, these homegrown red-eyes will almost always adjust to your care more easily than their wild-caught counterparts. It's important to only purchase sizable, well-established captive-bred red-eyed tree frogs, and to avoid freshly metamorphosed frogs less than 0.75 inches (1.9 cm) in length. At this small size, they tend to be very sensitive to stress and may succumb simply to the strain of being transported to so many different environments within a short period of time.

When wild-caught red-eyed tree frogs are the only option, it's important to carefully look over the frogs being purchased for any signs of illness or disease. Avoid red-eyed tree frogs with rostral abrasions or other superficial wounds—fairly common problems with red-eyes that have recently been imported. Bacterial infections also show up frequently in wild-caught red-eyed tree frogs. Look closely for any sores or unusual patches of skin that may indicate the presence of an infection. It's also a good idea to observe their behavior. When poked or disturbed while sleeping, a red-eyed tree frog should quickly open its eyes and be alert. Do not purchase an individual that reacts too slowly or in an odd way.

Housing

Red-eyed tree frogs should be kept in spacious enclosures that offer plenty of ventilation, and which are furnished heavily with large, broad-leaved plants. A group of three or four adult red-eyed tree frogs can be housed in a standard 20-gallon (76 L) aquarium or cage of equivalent size. They do not need to be housed in groups, and a smaller 10- or 15- gallon (38- or 57-L) aquarium is large enough for a single adult frog. Juveniles are best kept in plastic storage containers with ventilation holes drilled in the sides and cover, or in small 5.5 gallon (21-L) aquariums. These enclosures allow young frogs to easily hunt food until they are mature enough to manage a larger habitat.

Although the stereotypical image of the tropical rainforest in which red-eyed tree frogs live is of a very wet and humid place, red-eyed tree frogs spend much of their time exposed on leaves that receive lots of airflow and are not damp or overly wet. In captivity, this microclimate should be duplicated by providing a cage that is ventilated well. Glass or acrylic reptile and amphibian enclosures that have side vents for increased airflow are ideal.

Within the cage, a substrate and furnishings are needed. Lining the cage with slightly moist paper towels works well and makes cleaning the enclosure fast and simple. Many do not like the artificial appearance of paper towels so, if a more aesthetically pleasing substrate is desired, try moist sphagnum moss or ground coconut husk fiber, both of which retain moisture well and look natural. Bare-bottom setups can also be used.

Live or artificial plants should be placed to provide surfaces on which the frogs can rest during the day. If live plants are used, choose species with large, supportive leaves. These can be grown in pots and placed in or on the substrate so that they can be removed easily, which will make cleaning the cage easier. In addition to plants, a few driftwood or cork bark perches can be provided. These will be used at night, when the red-eyed tree frogs are on the hunt. A water bowl must also be offered to ensure the frogs stay hydrated.

Red-eyed tree frogs can also be housed in living terrariums, but they must not be overcrowded in these systems or too much waste will accumulate and throw off the balance within. Sturdy plants should be selected, because those with delicate leaves may be trampled during the night. The large amount of

Hands-Free Frogs

Red-eyed tree frogs do not tolerate handling well, and interactions with them should be limited to only when necessary. Frequently handled red-eyed tree frogs stress quickly and deteriorate in health.

Typical Panamanian red-eyed tree frog having dark red eyes and pale-colored sides.

ventilation red-eyed tree frogs require also may not be favorable to many of the common plants used in terrariums, which often like moist conditions. Plan well when building a terrarium for red-eyed tree frogs.

Temperature and Humidity

Keep red-eyed tree frogs warm, with a range of 75°F (24°C) to 85°F (29°C) being ideal during the day. At night, the terrarium should cool by 5°F to 10°F (3°C–6°C). If heating is needed, a small (usually 15- to 60-watt) infrared heat lamp can be used. As an alternative, if sphagnum moss or coconut husk fiber are used as substrates, a reptile heat pad can be attached underneath the cage.

Maintain high levels of humidity by misting the cage once a day, but do not allow the cage to become overly wet while misting because red-eyed tree frogs do not like living in excessively moist conditions. Instead, spray the cage lightly so that water evaporates over the following hour or two, providing a temporary increase in humidity during the day. Sometimes it's necessary to mist the cage several times a day if the frogs are kept in a room where the humidity is extremely low. Ideally, the humidity should range from 60 to 90 percent, sometimes climbing up to 100 percent directly following misting.

Diet

Red-eyed tree frogs can be maintained on a diet consisting largely of crickets. Feed adult frogs two to eight crickets a couple times a week. Juvenile red-eyed tree frogs grow best when fed daily, but take care not to feed too many food items at once or these young frogs may become stressed. In addition to crickets, offer red-eyed tree frogs other prey to vary

The author designed this living terrarium to house black-eyed tree frogs, and it would work for red-eyes as well.

their diet. Flying houseflies are relished by adults, and many will also accept small earthworms or silkworms offered in a dish at night. Cockroaches can be fed regularly, although only the juvenile roaches of the larger species will be accepted by red-eyed tree frogs. Supplement their food well with vitamin and calcium supplements.

Sexing

The size differential between male and female red-eyed tree frogs makes sexing them relatively easy. Male red-eyed tree frogs are smaller than adult females, and usually mature at 2.0 to 2.4 inches (5.0–6.0 cm), while females grow larger, to 2.4 to 2.8 inches (5.1–7.1 cm). A more accurate way to sex red-eyed tree frogs is to listen for the males, who will call at night when excited. In addition, male red-eyed tree frogs develop small, brown nuptial pads during the breeding season that easily distinguishes them from females.

Juvenile frogs cannot be sexed, so if breeding is the goal, and only juvenile frogs are available, it's best to purchase a large number to ensure you end up with at least a pair. They mature and are capable of breeding within 1 year.

Breeding

Like most tree frogs, red-eyed tree frogs breed during the wettest part of the year. This wet season usually follows a somewhat dry season in the wild, when temperatures are cool and the humidity remains low. To breed red-eyed tree frogs in captivity, most find it necessary to recreate these conditions.

Start by simulating the dry period. The temperature should remain cool, preferably somewhere between 70°F (21°C) and 80°F (27°C) during the day. In addition, the humidity level should be kept low. The substrate can be allowed to dry out, but always provide access to a bowl of water so that the frogs remain hydrated. It may also be helpful to cut back on feeding the frogs slightly, reducing both the quantity and frequency with which they are fed. The dry season can last 4 or more months in their native Central America, but captive red-eyed tree frogs may only need to be exposed to these dry and cool conditions for a few weeks to be prepared to breed.

Following the cool period, red-eyed tree frogs should be warmed back up, misted heavily, and fed frequently. Males will begin to call from elevated perches and, if fed well, the females will produce eggs. At this point, the frogs can be moved to a rain chamber, which should be fitted with broad-leaved plants suitable for females to deposit eggs on. In one night, females may lay multiple clutches, which can range in size from just 11 eggs to over 100. The number of eggs in most clutches usually falls somewhere between those two extremes. Sometimes eggs are laid on the side of the rain chamber instead of on plant leaves. These can be

Xanthic red-eyed tree frogs are mostly yellow with purplish sides. They are captive bred in small numbers.

removed with a smooth, flat, plastic object like a credit card, or can simply be left to develop in place, provided there is water below for the tadpoles to fall into.

Eggs that are deposited on plant leaves should be removed by snipping off the leaf on which they were laid. This should then be moved to a separate container and suspended a few inches above shallow water. Ensure that the humidity stays very high in this enclosure so that the eggs do not dry out. Alternatively, eggs on leaves can be left in the rain chamber, and the resulting tadpoles can be raised in the bottom water reservoir.

A week or so after the eggs were laid, tadpoles will start to emerge, falling down into the

Over-Eager Males

Male red-eyed tree frogs may sometimes amplex females who are not yet ready to breed. This can be stressful for the females so, if you notice a male grasping a female for more than a few days without any egg production, consider separating the two. It may be necessary to permanently house the two sexes separately if this behavior is repeated.

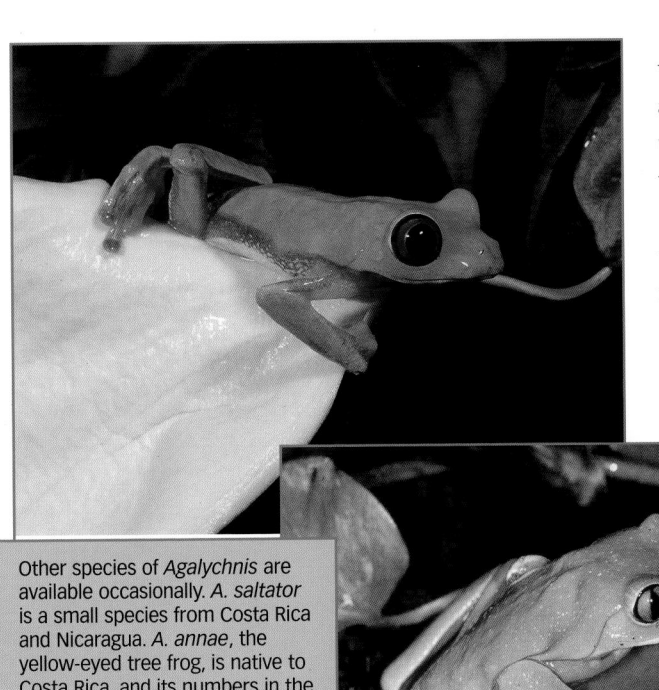

water below. Use a submersible aquarium heater with a thermostat to maintain a stable water temperature around 75°F (24°C). As the tadpoles mature, the water depth can be increased. Once the tadpoles are a week old and actively feeding, it may be preferable to move them to a different, established aquarium where they can continue to develop. The tadpoles will feed well on tropical fish flake, but may also rasp at algae that grows naturally in the aquarium.

In 1 to 2 months, most tadpoles should develop arms and complete their transformation into an arboreal frog. Newly morphed frogs will scale the glass to leave the water and can be plucked from the side of the aquarium and moved to a terrestrial setup as they are noticed. To prevent drowning, float a few pieces of cork bark in the water, or grow emergent plants that the frogs can use to climb out of the water. Keep newly metamorphosed frogs in simple setups, with a moist paper towel or bare bottom substrate, a potted plant for hiding, and a shallow water dish. Food for the young frogs should be composed largely of small crickets, although flightless fruit flies can be fed occasionally as well. The tiny red-eyed tree frogs are very fragile at this age, and it isn't unusual for a number of deaths to occur while they are maturing. However, if you are a conscientious keeper, most of your froglets should grow into healthy juveniles.

Other species of *Agalychnis* are available occasionally. *A. saltator* is a small species from Costa Rica and Nicaragua. *A. annae*, the yellow-eyed tree frog, is native to Costa Rica, and its numbers in the wild are declining.

Chapter 8

Monkey Frogs—
The Genus *Phyllomedusa*

Monkey frogs are some of the most fascinating tree frogs of all. Many people choose to work with these frogs because of their interesting breeding strategies and flashy contrasting colors. A couple species of *Phyllomedusa* are easy to care for, while others are more challenging to keep. With the proper knowledge and understanding of their captive care, monkey frogs are an excellent choice for the experienced tree-frog keeper.

Natural History

The South American genus *Phyllomedusa* contains some of the most bizarre and uniquely adapted of all tree frogs. There are 27 species within the genus, only one of which is not completely arboreal. The others spend all their adult life in trees and vegetation, even breeding above ground. To help them navigate their arboreal environment, *Phyllomedusa* species have evolved opposable, primate-like thumbs, hence the common name "monkey frogs."

Phyllomedusa species are often very striking in appearance, many with attractive, brightly colored markings concealed on the sides of their bodies and on the inner parts of their legs. Their appearance is enhanced as well by their bulging eyes, which look disproportionately large to their head and body.

An interesting and heavily studied feature of the genus *Phyllomedusa* is the diversity of chemicals produced by glands in their skin, and the interesting properties these substances possess. Most noteworthy are the variety of unique peptides, some of which are only produced by *Phyllomedusa* species and that have been found to be antimicrobial agents. Other chemical compounds produced by monkey tree frogs have different effects. The psychoactive skin secretions of the giant monkey tree frog (*P. bicolor*) are sometimes used by people indigenous to northern Peru to improve their senses prior to hunting.

Description of Available Species

Only a handful of monkey frogs appear in the pet trade. Most of these originate from the wild and are kept in captivity with limited to moderate success. Species that have been available in the recent past include: *P. bicolor*, Giant Monkey Frog; *P. burmeisteri*, Burmeister's Monkey Frog; *P. hypochondrialis*, Orange-legged Monkey Frog; *P. sauvagii*, Waxy Monkey Frog; *P. tarsius*, Brown-bellied Monkey Frog; *P. tomopterna*, Tiger-legged Monkey Frog; *P. vaillanti*, White-lined Monkey Frog.

Monkey frogs climb hand over hand along branches using their opposable thumbs, as this orange-legged monkey frog is doing.

Giant Monkey Frog

The largest member of *Phyllomedusa* is the giant monkey frog, *P. bicolor*. The smaller males generally mature to around 4.0 inches (10.2 cm) in length, while females can reach 4.7 inches (11.9 cm). They have a very robust appearance, with muscular limbs and a broad head. They are largely green, except for large white spots that border their reddish-brown ventral sides. The giant monkey frog is widespread throughout the Amazon basin, where it spends most of its time high in the canopy.

The giant monkey frog dwells high in the canopy of the Amazon, only descending to breed.

Those that appear in the pet trade are usually males that have been captured while descending to lower levels to breed during the rainy season. Occasionally females will be caught along with males. They make good captives when provided with a large enclosure and properly acclimated to captivity, but are not an easy species to accommodate or maintain because of their large size.

Burmeister's Monkey Frog

Burmeister's monkey frog (*P. burmeisteri*) is endemic to eastern Brazil. They are medium-sized frogs, reaching a maximum length of 3.2 inches (8.2 cm). Like other monkey frogs, their dorsal sides are usually green. The sides of their body are attractively spotted or barred

Waterproof Frogs

In addition to producing chemical compounds with psychoactive and antimicrobial properties, many species of *Phyllomedusa* have glands that secrete a wax-like substance composed largely of lipids. On hot or dry days, monkey frogs coat themselves in this substance to prevent water loss, effectively waterproofing themselves.

in yellow, beneath which is dark blue. This pattern continues along the inner sides of the arms and legs. Burmeister's monkey frog is uncommon in captivity, and only a handful of hobbyists currently keep them.

Orange-Legged Monkey Frog

The orange-legged monkey frog (*P. hypochondrialis*) is a smaller species of *Phyllomedusa* and ranges from 1.6 (4.0 cm) to 2.0 inches (5.0 cm) in length. Females are slightly larger than males. Their dorsal sides are green, with a white lateral stripe running down the sides of their bodies, sometimes wrapping around the front of the face. The inner sections of their limbs are striped in contrasting orange and black. This pattern continues through the sides of their bodies, but is usually concealed during the day when the frogs are asleep, having tucked their legs up tight against themselves.

The orange-legged monkey frog has a large range in South America, occupying much of Brazil, but also inhabiting countries as far north as Venezuela and as far south as Argentina. They are not canopy dwellers as some of the larger *Phyllomedusa* species are, but instead live among tall grasses, shrubs, and lower vegetation. Two subspecies exist, each hailing from different geographical areas. *P. hypochondrialis azurea* lives within the hot, arid Gran Chaco region of South America, while *P. hypochonrdrialis hypochondrialis* inhabits the wetter regions of the Amazon. In captivity, the orange-legged monkey frog has proved very hardy, and it is perhaps the most commonly available species in the pet trade.

Waxy Monkey Frog

The waxy monkey frog (*P. sauvagii*), also called the Chacoan monkey frog, is extremely well-adapted to cope with the dry, arid Chaco region of Argentina, Brazil, Bolivia, and Paraguay. Males grow to a maximum length of 2.8 inches (7.1 cm), while females are larger, capable of reaching 3.3 inches (8.2 cm). They are predominantly light green, with a thin white stripe wrapping around their lower lips and down the sides of their bodies. Thick white streaks are often found on the ventral surfaces.

Waxy monkey frogs have a stocky appearance. Two parotid glands protrude from the tops of their undersized heads, which look too small for their powerfully built bodies. Waxy monkey frogs coat themselves in a wax-like substance to prevent rapid water loss in their dry environment, hence their common name. In addition to this adaptation, they are capable of going without food for months at a time during the cool, dry winter to further cope with their harsh surroundings. In captivity, waxy monkey frogs make excellent captives, provided they are acquired in good health and their few basic needs are met.

Tiger-legged monkey frogs occur over much of the Amazon Basin.

Brown-Bellied Monkey Frog

The brown-bellied monkey frog (*P. tarsius*) grows large, ranging in size from 3.2 (8.1 cm) to 4.4 inches (11.2 cm). They can be found throughout rainforests in Brazil, Columbia, Ecuador, and Venezuela. Mainly green, the brown-bellied monkey frog has small, sometimes lightly colored bumps or nodules on the hind limbs and dorsum that give the skin a textured appearance. They are uncommon in captivity and, when they are available, they are not always in good condition, having recently arrived from their South American home. For this reason, the brown-bellied monkey frog is best left for experienced tree frog keepers.

Tiger-Legged Monkey Frog

The tiger-legged monkey frog (*P. tomopterna*) is a small- to medium-sized member of *Phyllomedusa*. As adults, males measure 1.6 to 1.9 inches (4.0 to 4.8 cm), while females are larger, growing to between 2.0 and 2.3 inches (5.2 to 5.9 cm). Like other monkey frogs, the dorsal coloration is green, which helps them blend into the leaves on which they sleep during the day. Hidden on the sides of their bodies and insides of their legs are very attractive orange and black stripes. These stripes can be seen when the frog is awake and active. The common names tiger-striped monkey frog and barred monkey frog are also used to refer to *P. tomopterna*.

They occupy a very large range within the Amazon, through much of northern Brazil and surrounding countries. There, tiger-legged monkey frogs spend their time high above ground in trees. In captivity, they do well once acclimated but are notorious for arriving in poor shape when imported and needing special attention during the initial acclimation period.

White-Lined Monkey Frog

The white-lined monkey frog (*P. vaillanti*) grows to between 2.0 and 3.3 inches (5.0 to 8.4 cm). Predominantly green, the white-lined monkey frog has a very angular body structure. Two dotted white lines extend from their heads down their backs, emphasizing this. Yellow blotches run along their flanks, bordering their ventral sides.

The waxy monkey frog has large parotid glands, although all the species produce toxic secretions.

Like the brown-bellied monkey frog, the white-lined monkey frog has somewhat textured skin, with fleshy bumps covering its limbs. Wild-caught individuals are infrequently available and must be cared for with great attention because, like other monkey frogs, the white-lined monkey frog can be very sensitive while acclimating to captivity.

Acquisition

Always purchase captive-bred monkey frogs when available to avoid the hassle and difficulty of acclimating wild ones to captivity. The waxy monkey frog and orange-legged monkey frog are bred more frequently than other species, and captive-bred offspring of both can be located from dealers and breeders with some frequency. Less commonly bred is the tiger-legged monkey frog. Burmeister's monkey frog has only recently become available and is not common, although it too has been bred in captivity. The other three *Phyllomedusa* species mentioned are rarely bred, with wild-caught individuals often being the only available option to their prospective keepers.

Wild-caught monkey frogs are notorious for arriving from their origin in poor shape, heavily stressed and parasitized, and often with injuries like rostral abrasions and other trauma. Bacterial infections show up somewhat frequently as well. Monitor all wild-caught monkey frogs carefully in large, well-ventilated, hygienic setups. Contact a veterinarian who can prescribe medication to treat some of the ailments that often arise when dealing with wild-caught monkey frogs. Stress is a large problem for frogs that have recently been imported, so avoid interaction between established pet frogs and fresh imports.

Housing

Small species, like the orange-legged monkey frog, can be maintained well in aquariums with screen covers. A standard 10- or 20-gallon (38- or 76-L) aquarium can be used to house several individuals. The larger monkey frogs need more room, with the largest of the bunch, the giant monkey frog, requiring a cage several feet (1 m or more) in width, length, and height.

Ventilation is of utmost importance. Perched high in trees, monkey frogs are constantly exposed to the elements. Provide them with similar conditions in captivity by using a screen cover, or even better, buying or constructing a cage that has ventilation in both the top and sides to allow for maximum airflow. Screen cages can also be used to house monkey frogs, provided they are not made out of an abrasive material.

The substrate and furnishings within the cage need not be complex. Simple substrates such as paper towels, upholstery foam rubber, or bare-bottom setups all work well. Ground coconut husk fiber and sphagnum moss are good choices for a more natural appearance and for those species from humid regions.

Provide plenty of foliage and cover in the form of potted live plants. This is particularly important for species that rest on leaves during the day, such as the tiger-

Because they are hardy and often available as captive-bred juveniles, orange-legged monkey frogs are good for first-time keepers.

legged monkey frog and white-lined monkey frog. Sturdy perches and climbing branches should also be made available, especially for the giant monkey frog and waxy monkey frog, both of which don't generally spend their time on leaves, but instead sit on the branches of trees. Sections of PVC plastic pipe can be secured in place for sturdy and easily cleaned perches. Cork bark tubes and driftwood also work well. A large, shallow water dish should always be provided so that the frogs can stay hydrated.

Temperature and Humidity

Different temperature ranges are necessary for different monkey frogs. The waxy monkey frog and Chacoan orange-legged monkey frog (*P. hypochondrialis azurea*) live in the hot Gran Chaco region of South America. For these two species, part of the cage should reach 90°F to 95°F (32°C–35°C) during the day, with the ambient temperature in the rest of their environment hovering around 80°F (27°C). These conditions can be created by positioning an incandescent light bulb above one end of the cage, creating a warm area directly below it. At night, this bulb should be shut off to provide a drop in temperature, preferably down to around 70°F (21°C).

The other monkey frogs discussed in this chapter inhabit different parts of South America, and are not exposed to such an extreme range of temperatures. They do well with a temperature that varies within the cage from around 75°F (24°C) to 82°F (28°C) during the day, dropping slightly at night.

Most monkey frogs should be kept in a reasonably humid environment. Misting the cage once or twice daily will help maintain a high humidity level, but take care not to mist too heavily because you don't want to soak the cage. The waxy monkey frog and Chacoan orange-legged monkey frog inhabit arid parts of South America and should be kept dry, only having their cage misted with water every now and then or to induce breeding.

Diet

The larger species of monkey frogs can be maintained on a diet consisting largely of adult crickets and cockroaches. Moths or other large prey can be offered occasionally to vary their diet. The smaller monkey frogs are not large enough to consume adult roaches but will feed well on crickets. Occasionally, earthworms can be offered in a dish at night, and houseflies, moths, and other flying insects can be released into their cage to add some variation as well. Juvenile monkey frogs should be fed in small quantities daily, while adults do best if fed once every 2 to 5 days. Use high-quality vitamin and calcium supplements on their food to ensure that all nutritional requirements are met.

Giant monkey frogs need larger and sturdier climbing branches than most other tree frogs.

Breeding

Only a couple species of monkey frogs are bred in captivity with any frequency, with the others usually only breeding when wild-caught, preconditioned pairs are obtained and placed directly into a rain chamber. In part, the scarcity of captive breeding of certain species may be due to the lack of availability of healthy individuals that acclimate well to captivity.

The two species most often bred are those from the arid Gran Chaco region: the waxy monkey frog and the Chacoan orange-legged monkey frog. Of the monkey frogs from the Amazon, the orange-legged monkey frog and tiger-legged monkey frog are most often bred.

Sexing

Adult monkey frogs are easily sexed because males are usually smaller than females. Male monkey frogs that have been captured during the breeding season often have developed dark, rough-looking nuptial pads at the base of their

Orange-Leg Origins

The orange-legged monkey frog occupies a very large range in South America, with populations found in both dry, arid environments and humid rainforests. When keeping this species, it's important to find out where the individuals you acquire originate from and which subspecies they are. *P. hypochondrialis azurea* from the Gran Chaco region should be kept hot and dry, while *P. hypochondrialis hypochondrialis* from the Amazon does best in cooler, more humid conditions.

Mysterious Monkeys

The giant monkey frog has proved difficult to breed, even when exposed to strong cycles and conditions in which other captive monkey frogs regularly reproduce. This suggests that there might be something we're missing, some aspect of their breeding behavior that has yet to be understood, and leaves plenty of room for prospective tree-frog breeders to experiment.

forearm. In addition, male monkey frogs that have been calling excessively usually have a slightly darkened throat. Wild-caught monkey frogs are most often males that have descended to lower vegetation to breed, and finding females can sometimes be problematic.

Conditioning

Breeding monkey frogs involves the usual replication of wet and dry seasons. This can be accomplished by allowing their terrarium to dry for several weeks by cutting back on misting so that the humidity level is lowered. Both the waxy monkey frog and Chacoan orange-legged monkey frog are normally kept in dry conditions and, for both of these species, it is usually only necessary to cool the terrarium slightly for a few weeks to precondition them to breed. Following the artificial dry season, the temperature and humidity should be increased, and the frogs should be fed heavily, being offered a variety of food items.

Once males begin to call and females look fat, the frogs can be moved to a rain chamber. Small species do not require large rain chambers, and a simple 15- or 20-gallon (57- or 76-l) aquarium may suffice. The larger monkey frogs are best bred in larger rain chambers, such as modified shower stalls, or large, vertically oriented aquariums. The pump that powers the spray bar can be set to turn on periodically throughout the later half of the day and night. If all goes well, males will amplex the females. When females are not ready to

Male waxy monkey frog calling in Paraguay. This species breeds readily in captivity.

A pair of white-lined monkey frogs in amplexus. This species is challenging to breed.

breed or have not produced eggs, males will often ride around on their back, amplexing them for multiple days without successfully breeding. If the frogs do not spawn after several days of amplexus, separate them for a few weeks, feed heavily, and then reintroduce them to the rain chamber.

Wild monkey frogs wrap their eggs within plant leaves that overhang water so, within the rain chamber, suitably positioned plants should be provided. The Chacoan orange-legged monkey frog (*P. hypochondrialis azurea*) will use both pothos (*Scindapsus* sp.) and small philodendrons to wrap their eggs, but larger species do best when provided with larger leaves for breeding. Clutch size varies between species, from as little as a few dozen eggs (*P. hypochondrialis*) to over one thousand (*P. bicolor*). The leaf they are wrapped in should be removed to a separate cage and suspended above water, much in the same way as you would the eggs of the red-eyed tree frog. It's important that the humidity in this enclosure housing the folded leaf and eggs remains high so that the eggs do not dry out.

As tadpoles break free from the egg mass, they drop into the water below, where they begin their aquatic life stage. Tadpoles can be maintained as described in the breeding chapter of this book. The water should be heated with a submersible aquarium heater to around 78°F (26°C). Monkey frogs usually metamorphose in 1 to 2 months at this temperature, but this may vary some between species. Young, freshly morphed monkey frogs are delicate, and should be carefully cared for in a similar way to the adults, except they must be fed more frequently and kept in smaller enclosures so that they can locate food easily.

Chapter 9

White's Tree Frog

Possibly the best tree frog suited for captivity is White's tree frog, Litoria *caerulea*. This hefty Australian native is a regular in pet stores—and for good reason. They make extraordinary pets, being hardy enough for the novice tree frog keeper, yet rewarding for just about anyone to care for, including professionals and experts. White's tree frogs are also one of the few tree frogs bred consistently in captivity, and captive-bred stock is regularly available from many different sources, adding to the reasons they make superb pets.

Description

As adults, White's tree frogs grow large and are capable of reaching 3.9 inches (10.0 cm) in length. They are very robust, with strong, thick legs, which they use to move their round, heavyset body. Most are uniform in color and have little in the way of patterns or markings, with their dorsal side ranging from solid green, to brown, to turquoise depending on the environmental conditions to which they are exposed and the origin of the frog. Some White's tree frogs are speckled in small white or yellowish dots. In captivity, at least two lines of White's tree frog exist, one originating from Australia, which tends to look more blue or turquoise in color, the other from Indonesia and most often appearing light green.

Australian White's tree frogs are often bluish in color.

Natural History

White's tree frog belongs to the genus *Litoria*, which contains around 130 species, all of which are native to Australia, Indonesia, and surrounding island countries. White's tree frog itself has a wide distribution, occupying much of the northeast half of Australia. Scattered populations also inhabit New Guinea and Indonesia to the north. They can be found in many different habitats, from woodlands, to grasslands, and even urban areas, where they've been known to take up residence in gardens, cisterns, bathrooms, and even mailboxes!

The Name Game

In addition to being called White's tree frog, *L. caerulea* is also often referred to as the dumpy tree frog or green tree frog.

A common misconception is that the common name "White's tree frog" has something to do with the color of *L. caerulea*. In fact, it instead refers to the man who first described the species, John White.

Captive Care

White's tree frog is one of the hardiest tree frogs available. They are adaptable to many different keeping conditions, making them excellent for first-time frog keepers.

Acquisition

There are many different places to purchase White's tree frogs, and they are commonly available as young, captive-bred frogs and larger, wild-caught adults. Always opt for captive-bred frogs when possible. Although usually more expensive, they are normally in better health than those that are wild-caught. Pet stores regularly carry captive-bred White's tree frogs and are a good source for them because they provide the opportunity to inspect the frogs in person before making the purchase. White's tree frogs can also be located relatively easily at reptile shows, as well as on the Internet through dealers.

Housing

A standard 20- or 30- gallon (76- or 114-L) aquarium is large enough for a pair or trio of White's tree frogs. Although they remain asleep during the day and may appear inactive, at night they will move about and use all the room provided to them. Juveniles can be raised in smaller 5- or 10-gallon (19- or 38-L) aquariums until they grow large enough to be moved to a bigger tank. Always use a screen cover on aquariums to provide plenty of ventilation. As an alternative to an aquarium, large plastic storage bins can be used, as long as they are modified to provide good airflow.

Many different substrates work well for White's tree frogs. The

A White's tree frog emerging from a tree hole in Kakadu National Park, Australia.

most practical are paper towels or upholstery foam rubber, both of which are cheap and can be changed with ease. If either substrate is used, keep the rest of the cage setup simple so that the necessary frequent cleanings can easily be done. Ground coconut husk fiber, soil mixtures, and high-quality sphagnum moss are three other good options for a substrate, and these give the cage a more natural appearance.

In addition to a substrate, cage furnishings are needed.

Driftwood or cork bark can be placed leaning against the side of the cage to provide hiding areas, and artificial plants can be used to offer cover as well as climbing areas at night. To complete the setup, provide a large water dish to allow the frogs to soak and stay hydrated. This must be changed daily.

Temperature and Humidity

One of the best qualities of White's tree frogs is their ability to tolerate a wide range of temperatures. Ideally, the temperature in the cage should range from 75°F to 85°F (24°C to 29°C) during the day, with a slight drop in temperature at night. They are very tolerant of temperatures outside this range though, so occasional cool or hot days don't usually present a problem. If heating is needed, a small infrared heat lamp can be placed above one end of the cage. In addition to providing heat, this also allows you to view the frogs at night without disturbing them.

Being native to grasslands and wooded areas in Australia, White's tree frogs do not require constant high humidity. Instead, they should be maintained in a moderately humid environment, with average household humidity levels usually suiting them well. During dry parts of the year, when humidity levels are low, their cage can be misted with water to temporarily increase the humidity within. Allow the cage to remain humid and moist directly after being misted, but not wet, and never allow the substrate to become waterlogged or fully saturated with water.

Diet

White's tree frogs have a huge appetite and are ready for a meal practically anytime. Watching them greedily stuff food into their mouths is entertaining, and

White's tree frogs will thrive in living terrariums, but they may trample fragile plants.

often somewhat disturbing as the cute pet frog you once thought you were caring for turns into a viscous predator, leaping across the cage to consume an unlucky insect. Their diet should largely be composed of crickets. Around a half dozen should be fed to adult frogs twice a week, occasionally feeding in smaller or larger amounts. Feed juvenile White's tree frogs daily.

Voracious predators, White's tree frogs will eat anything they can cram in their mouths—in this case, a small snake.

In addition to crickets, offer cockroaches, moths, houseflies, super worms, wax worms, silkworms, and earthworms to vary their diet. Adult White's tree frogs also readily feed on live baby mice, although these should be fed sparingly. Supplement their food with high-quality calcium and vitamin supplements. This is particularly important for young, growing White's tree frogs, whose food should be lightly coated in a supplement at nearly every feeding.

Breeding

When properly conditioned, White's tree frogs are relatively easy to breed. They are a good choice for a first breeding project, but be prepared because a single successful breeding can yield thousands of tadpoles.

Sexing

White's tree frogs are not as easy to sex as many other species of tree frogs. Sometimes a slight size difference is noted between adult males and females, with females being somewhat larger than males. The difference is not always noticeable though, so it's helpful to use other cues as well. Males that have been calling excessively normally have a darkened throat. In addition, those that are in breeding condition develop dark nuptial pads at the base of their thumbs and, if these are present, it's a sure sign that the frog is a male.

Both male and female White's tree frogs vocalize so, unlike many other commonly kept species, a calling frog isn't necessarily a male. Female White's tree frogs usually call in response to hearing a male, and do so for much shorter periods of time. By observing their behavior while vocalizing it's often possible to differentiate between males and females, with the males sending out their loud advertisement call usually perched high in the cage, while the shyer females are either silent or emit a few croaks here and there in response.

Conditioning

White's tree frogs must be properly conditioned to breed in captivity. This period of conditioning can be stressful, so make sure only healthy frogs with good weight are exposed to it. Start by letting the terrarium cool until the temperature in the tank rarely rises above 70°F (21°C). Allow the humidity level in the cage to decrease as well, but ensure a source of clean water is always available for the frogs to soak in so that they can stay hydrated. During this period, feedings can be cut back, and even stopped all together once the coldest part of this simulated winter is reached.

If you live in a temperate region, it is easiest to condition frogs during the winter months when your house naturally cools and the air becomes dry. A cool basement may work well for conditioning White's tree frogs as well. This artificial winter should last for about 6 weeks or slightly longer, after which time the frogs can slowly be warmed back up to their normal temperatures and feeding schedule.

The Rain Chamber

Once the frogs are again exposed to their normal conditions, increase the frequency with which they are misted. In addition, it's very important that they are fed heavily. If all goes well, male White's tree frogs begin to call each night, with interested females softly responding back. At this point, the frogs can be moved to a large rain chamber with a few inches of water in the bottom, floating pieces of cork bark, and aquatic vegetation. A large piece of driftwood or two should extend out of the water to provide perches for the tree frogs.

Heat the water with a submersible aquarium heater so that the temperature within the rain chamber stays on the warm side of their temperature range, about 85°F (29°C). The pump that powers the rain bar above the frogs should be set to go on periodically throughout the day and night. Continue feeding heavily in the rain

In Distress

Both males and females will emit a distress call when they feel threatened, such as when they are handled or disturbed. This should not be confused with other vocalization and cannot be used a means to sex them.

Because they are hardy and easily bred, White's tree frogs are ideal for first-time frog breeders.

chamber, but make sure to remove dead feeder insects to maintain good water quality. Breeding will usually take place at night, during which thousands of eggs are laid on the water surface, slowly sinking to the bottom the following day.

Egg and Tadpole Care

The eggs can be allowed to develop in the water that fills the bottom of the rain chamber until tadpoles hatch. If the rain chamber is large enough, and there are only a few hundred tadpoles, they can be raised within it until they metamorphose. Larger numbers of tadpoles are best moved to aquariums or plastic stock tanks. Maintain a water temperature between 80°F (27°C) and 85°F (29°C), and feed the tadpoles daily with high-quality fish flake.

Tadpoles metamorphose between 4 and 6 weeks at these temperatures. As soon as they develop arms, it's possible for the tailed frogs to drown so, at this point, they should be provided with floating plants, cork bark slabs, or rocks that emerge from the water so that they can climb out with ease. The tiny White's tree frogs can then be moved to a simple setup, using either a bare-bottom or paper towels as a substrate, a few live or artificial plants, and a shallow water dish. Start feeding the young, growing frogs daily a few days after their tails are absorbed. Initially, feed them small crickets until they put on a little size, at which point they can be offered houseflies and other food items to vary their diet.

Two Bloodlines

An effort should be made to keep the blue or turquoise-colored Australian White's tree frogs from breeding with the more common green Indonesian White's to preserve the two separate lines.

Chapter 10

Other Tree Frogs

t's no surprise that, with over 1,000 species of tree frogs, others show up in the pet trade in addition to the small handful mentioned in previous chapters. It's not possible to cover all within this book, but included in this chapter are short summaries of some of the more frequently encountered tree frogs not yet discussed.

Cuban Tree Frog

The Cuban tree frog (*Osteopilus septentrionalis*) is the largest tree frog found in North America, with large females reported at over 5.0 inches (12.7 cm) in length. Most are smaller however, and males may mature when only 1.5 inches (3.8 cm) long. The color of Cuban tree frogs is quite variable, and they are capable of changing from white, to tan, to green depending on the environmental conditions to which they are exposed. A spotted or blotchy pattern is often present, although sometimes it isn't apparent when Cuban tree frogs are very a light or dark color.

Cuban tree frogs are robust amphibians, capable of catching and eating small mammals, birds, and other frogs.

Natural History

Cuban tree frogs have proved adaptable to many different environments and can be found in a variety habitats. They can thrive as long as there is a source of water available and the temperature is warm enough. This is a great quality for a pet amphibian, but has caused many problems for native frogs in areas where the Cuban tree frog has accidentally been released.

These frogs are native to Cuba and surrounding islands, but can now be found in Florida, southern Georgia, Hawaii, and even Costa Rica. In Florida—and presumably the other areas where the Cuban tree frog has been introduced—native amphibians have borne the brunt of this invasion. Cuban tree frogs love to dine on other frogs, and they will even eat smaller individuals of their own species. In addition, they are able to produce a toxic secretion that prevents the normal predators in the area from consuming them. This has thrown off the natural balance of the ecosystems invaded by Cuban tree frogs and is a large cause of concern.

Keep Track of Your Frogs

If you choose to keep Cuban tree frogs, and you live in an environment suitable for them to inhabit, be very careful not to release any. You may even consider keeping a different species of tree frog to prevent any accidental releases.

Care

In captivity, Cuban tree frogs are both hardy and easily kept. They are a fine choice for a first tree frog because of these two qualities. Cuban tree frogs are very fast, and can be somewhat nervous captives, but they demand few special requirements. Although groups of Cuban tree frogs can be kept together provided they are all a similar size, they should not be kept with other frogs because of their cannibalistic behavior and harmful skin secretions.

Acquisition All Cuban tree frogs available in the pet trade are wild-caught and, because they are both inexpensive and common, they are not always well-cared for. Their jumpy disposition means that while being stocked in small enclosures they often bruise or damage themselves trying to escape. Carefully inspect the frogs for injuries when selecting one. Pass up any Cuban tree frog that is sleeping on the ground or is otherwise behaving strangely.

Housing Complex cage setups are not necessary for Cuban tree frogs. They are large and robust and may trample small plants or cage furnishings, so a simple, hygienic setup with sturdy perches and resting spots works best.

A standard 20-gallon (76-L) aquarium is large enough for a small group of Cuban tree frogs. I don't recommend attempting to permanently house them in smaller enclosures because of their nervous temperament and active behavior. They can also be housed successfully in plastic storage containers with ventilation holes drilled in the sides and cover. Tape an aquarium background to the exterior of three sides of the enclosure to make your frogs feel more secure.

Moist paper towels or upholstery foam rubber are excellent substrates for Cuban tree frogs. For a more natural appearance, use wetted sphagnum moss or ground coconut husk fiber instead. Within the cage, a few branching pieces of driftwood or cork bark tubes can be positioned to form sturdy perches that the frogs will climb on during the night. In addition, artificial plants can be used to offer hiding areas and additional surfaces on which to climb. Hardy live plants with supportive leaves, such as pothos (*Scindapsus aureus*) or small *Calathea* species, can be used as well, but should be grown in pots as opposed to soil within the cage, to make cleaning and maintenance easier.

Messy Frogs

Because of their large size, Cuban tree frogs can be somewhat messy. It is to your advantage to design a cage setup that is easy to maintain so that it can be cleaned without difficulty.

Multiple Names

In addition to the common name Amazonian milk frog, *T. resinifictrix* is often found for sale under other names, such as milky tree frog, Brazilian cave frog, and panda bear tree frog. Further complicating matters, until recently, the Amazonian milk frog was assigned to the genus *Phrynohyas*, which is now considered synonymous with *Trachycephalus*. *Trachycephalus* contains only ten species, all of which are native to Central and South America.

A large water dish must be provided for Cuban tree frogs to soak in. They will use this every night, and it should be changed the following morning to prevent the buildup of waste.

Cuban tree frogs do best when kept warm, with the ideal daytime temperature ranging from 78°F (26°C) to 88°F (31°C). At night, the temperature can be reduced 5°F to 10°F (3°C–6°C). The humidity should also be kept high, which can be achieved by misting the cage with water once a day and restricting ventilation if necessary.

Diet Their large appetite and energetic feeding response is one of the most enjoyable qualities of Cuban tree frogs. They will consume pretty much anything that moves and can fit into their mouths, including other frogs and small lizards. In captivity, a healthy diet should consist largely of appropriately sized crickets, although cockroaches may be a good alternative staple diet. Feed a few of these every couple days. In addition, wax worms, super worms, silkworms, and even newborn pinky mice can be offered occasionally to vary their diet. Proper supplementation is important, so use the correct calcium and vitamin supplements to ensure that nutritional requirements are met.

Breeding

Cuban tree frogs are not bred in captivity frequently, if at all, and for good reason. They are an invasive species in much of their range, and it is possible to collect them in large numbers without worrying about negatively altering their native wild populations. There are already too many Cuban tree frogs in places they shouldn't be, making them one of the few species I would discourage most from attempting to breed.

In the wild, Cuban tree frogs reproduce in large numbers. A single female may produce a clutch containing thousands of eggs, which she will then distribute in partial clutches around the water's surface. Tadpoles are cannibalistic and will consume each other in addition to algae and plant life. They can metamorphose in less than 1 month.

Amazonian Milk Frog

Amazonian milk frogs and other *Trachycephalus* are strongly arboreal, even breeding in the canopy within holes in trees.

The canopy-dwelling Amazonian milk frog (*Trachycephalus resinifictrix*) has a large range throughout the Amazon, from Ecuador and Peru, east through Brazil, and north to French Guiana and Venezuela. They rarely, if ever, descend to the ground, even breeding within water-filled hollows in trees. Males defend large territories in their arboreal environment, calling loudly from inside tree holes. Duellman reports population densities as low as one male every 20 to 25 hectares in Peru, which is a very large area for a single male frog to occupy.

Adult male Amazonian milk frogs mature to around 2.5 inches (6.4 cm), while females grow larger and range in size from 3.5 to 4.0 inches (8.9 cm to 10.2 cm). They have very large toe pads and strong limbs, which help them climb and move about in the trees in which they live. Their heads are blunt and rounded in appearance, and on top sit large, light orange-colored eyes. Juveniles are striped in contrasting white and charcoal gray, with their limbs being sharply banded in these two colors, and their dorsum and heads being more loosely patterned. As they mature, Amazonian milk frogs lose this contrasting appearance as the white darkens and the gray lightens. In addition, their skin take on a more textured appearance, eventually being covered in small bumps. Adults are colored more evenly, and are largely grayish brown, with faint banding still noticeable, particularly on the limbs. Sometimes the bands are broken into spots or swirls. Small tan dots cover the grays and browns, creating an intricate and complex pattern.

Care

Only recently becoming widely available, Amazonian milk frogs are well-suited for captivity. They make good pets because of their attractive appearance and ease of care. Author and experienced amphibian keeper Danté Fenolio has compared their captive requirements to that of White's tree frog, which is well-known for being one of the most easily kept and adaptable tree frogs in captivity. Nearly all Amazonian milk frogs in the pet trade are the product of captive breeding, so healthy, captive-bred frogs are easily located.

The milk frogs are named for the copious milky toxins they secrete when attacked, as this *T. venulosus* is doing.

Amazonian milk frogs can be purchased from a number of sources. They are not as commonly available through pet stores as many other tree frogs are. Instead, the best place to locate them is through reptile and amphibian dealers on the Internet or at local reptile and amphibian shows.

A standard 20- or 30-gallon (76- or 113.5-l) aquarium fitted with a screen cover is large enough for an adult trio of milk frogs. Amazonian milk frogs are highly arboreal animals, so it's important to choose an enclosure that has plenty of height and offers ample climbing space. Younger animals are best kept in a smaller enclosure, such as a 10-gallon (38-l) aquarium, plastic cage, or storage container of equivalent size. The young frogs will be able to find food more easily in the smaller enclosure, which should be upgraded to a larger one as they grow.

Possible substrates include a bare-bottom, damp paper towels, upholstery foam rubber, ground coconut husk fiber, or high-quality sphagnum moss. The latter two will create a more aesthetically pleasing environment. High in the canopy of the rain forests of South America, Amazonian milk frogs spend much of their time tucked away within holes in trees. Although it's not necessary to replicate this in captivity, providing artificial tree holes for milk frogs can add a nice touch. Cork bark tubes are a simple way to offer secluded hiding spots for the frogs to rest in during the day. A less natural, but more easily cleaned and practical approach, is to use sections of PVC pipe of a suitable diameter.

Sturdy live or artificial plants can also be used within the cage for cover. Pieces of driftwood or cork bark should be provided as perches and shelter in addition to plants. To complete the cage setup, place a large water dish in it.

Temperature and Humidity

Amazonian milk frogs are best kept in an enclosure that is maintained between 75°F (24°C) and 85°F (29°C) during the day, cooling by several degrees at night. They will tolerate temperatures outside of this range well but, like most tree frogs, should not be exposed to drafty conditions where the temperature fluctuates

often. Although they are from tropical regions, high humidity does not seem to be necessary to keep them in good health, and they will do well when kept in environments maintained at many different humidity levels. Misting the cage with water a few times a week will help keep the substrate moist and bring about beneficial temporary increases in humidity.

Diet The Amazonian milk frog is a large tree frog with an equally large appetite. They eat most commonly available live feeders, including crickets, cockroaches, silkworms, earthworms, and moths. Adults will also consume newborn mice. Crickets should form the majority of their diet, with other food items offered every few feedings to add variety. Adult frogs can be fed

Juvenile Amazonian milk frogs (top) have a more contrasting and attractive pattern than the adults (bottom), although some adults retain some of the juvenile colors.

two times a week, while juveniles are best fed daily if possible. Like most tree frogs, Amazonian milk frogs are nocturnal and should be fed at night when they are active.

Breeding

Tree holes are the only place in which Amazonian milk frogs are known to breed in the wild. Males call relentlessly through the night during the rainy season to attract mates and defend territory from other males. Females join successful males within water-filled holes, where breeding takes place. Clutch size can vary from around 100 eggs to well over 1,000. Tadpoles develop in the water within the tree hollow, where they feed largely on eggs from the parents, who breed multiple times during the rainy season. Decomposing debris and algae are consumed as well. After a couple months, the tadpoles complete metamorphosis and climb out of the hole and into their new arboreal environment, never having touched ground.

To breed the Amazonian milk frog in captivity, it is necessary to replicate the conditions that they experience in the wild, most notably the rainy season and the presence of tree holes. At the time of this writing, most Amazonian milk frogs available originate from only a couple sources, so captive breeding is still not widely achieved. Coupled with their fascinating breeding strategy, the infrequency with which they are bred should encourage others to give breeding a try and further increase the availability of this superb pet tree frog.

Sexing The easiest way to distinguish between the sexes is by size. Males are noticeably smaller than females. In addition, males call loudly at night, so if your frog is vocalizing it's a sure sign it is a male. Like most tree frogs, the nuptial pads found at the base of the thumb on male frogs will become noticeable during the breeding season and are another reliable way to tell males apart from females. Juvenile frogs cannot be sexed.

The Rain Chamber and Artificial Tree Hole
The rain chamber for Amazonian milk frogs should be somewhat different from those used for other frogs. Rather than allowing water to pool in the bottom, as you would for many other tree frogs, it may be helpful to fit the rain chamber with a drain and sump in which a pump and aquarium heater can sit. This will limit the available body of water in the rain chamber to an artificial tree hole that you create, which is where the frogs will breed.

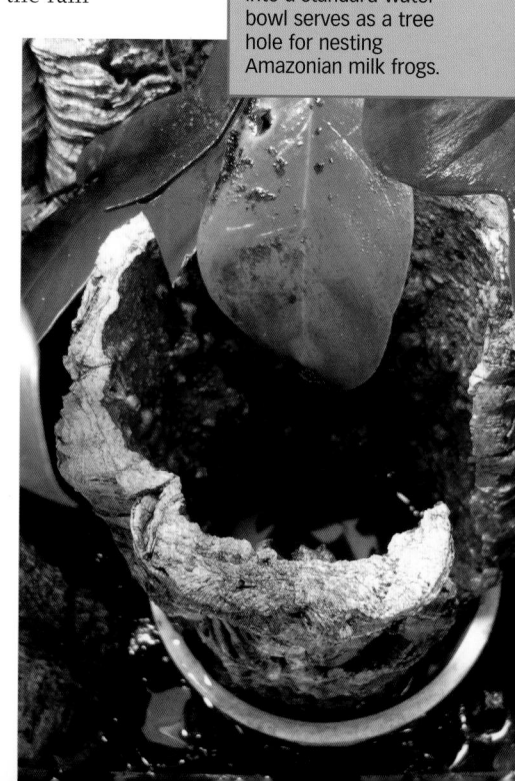

A cork bark tube inserted into a standard water bowl serves as a tree hole for nesting Amazonian milk frogs.

An alternative to using a drain and sump is to create a false bottom. See the housing chapter for details on false bottoms. This technique raises the floor of the enclosure above the water level. It should tightly fit the dimensions of the rain chamber so that the frogs cannot climb under it, where the water, pump, and aquarium heater are. No substrate is needed over the false bottom.

An artificial, water-filled tree hole is usually necessary to breed milk frogs. In 1996, the first successful captive breeding was achieved by the Amphibia Research Group, and it occurred using a small plastic storage container as a tree hole. The container was modified by cutting a hole into the cover, which allowed the tree frogs to enter. In addition, smaller holes were cut in the sides of the container so that excess water could drain out as it rained in from above.

Another type of artificial tree hole can be constructed out of a large cork-bark tube and water dish. By taking one end of the cork bark tube and wedging it into a water dish of suitable diameter, a deep, cylindrical tree hole can be created. Within the dish, a few inches of water should be present. This technique has been used to breed the crowned tree frog, *Anotheca spinosa*, and it would likely work for *T. resinifictrix* as well. There are other ways to create suitable breeding holes for milk frogs, and it's worth experimenting to develop your own method. Sometimes Amazonian milk frogs in breeding condition will simply spawn in water dishes placed in the rain chamber, so an artificial tree hole is not always necessary. Experiment with your frogs to see if they will adapt to this less complicated setup.

Tadpole Care If breeding is successful, you will notice eggs floating on the surface of the water. As tadpoles develop and break away from the gelatinous egg mass, they initially float, suspended near the top of the water. At this point, they should be moved to an aquarium, fitted with the proper filtration and a submersible aquarium heater to maintain the appropriate water temperature. Although wild tadpoles often feed primarily on other eggs deposited in their tree hole by the parents, captive tadpoles will grow well when fed high-quality tropical fish flake. Perform partial water changes frequently, particularly if you have a large number of tadpoles in the aquarium. Tadpoles complete metamorphosis and emerge from the water between 5.5 and 8 weeks at a water temperature of 78°F (26°C).

Clown Tree Frog

The clown tree frog (*Dendropsophus leucophyllatus*) is a charming little frog. They inhabit areas around bodies of water in the Amazon Basin, from Peru east through Brazil and surrounding countries. They stay small, with males growing to only around 1.3 inches (3.3 cm). Females are larger, and can reach 1.7 inches (4.4 cm) in length. Clown tree frogs are attractively patterned. Their dorsum have maroon to dark brown hourglass-shaped markings, which are surrounded by a soft yellow to gold color. This yellow is also present on their burgundy and red limbs. At night, clown tree frogs lighten and look ghostly in appearance. Additional color forms exist, but these are not often seen in captivity.

The clown tree frog occurs in two very different patterns, the clown phase and the reticulated or giraffe phase. The giraffe phase is rare in the herp hobby.

Care

Their small size and colorful appearance make clown tree frogs highly desirable pets. Most found for sale are wild-caught and need to be monitored closely while they acclimate to captivity but, once adjusted, they do very well. A standard 10- or 15-gallon (38- or 57-l) aquarium is large enough for a group of five frogs. Sphagnum moss, ground coconut husk fiber, or soil mixtures all work well as substrates. Moist paper towels can be used as an alternative, as long as they are changed regularly.

When captive clown tree frogs are disturbed during the day, they have a tendency to jump from their arboreal perch down to the ground, where they will hide beneath anything that is available until they feel secure again. To accommodate this behavior, you may want to place a handful of leaf litter over the substrate so the frogs have something to hide underneath when frightened. In addition, provide plenty of cover in the form of live plants, as well as a large water dish for soaking at night.

The cage can be maintained between 75°F (24°C) and 82°F (28°C) during the day, cooling slightly at night. These moderate temperatures should be accompanied by relatively high humidity most of the time. Crickets can be fed a couple times a week, offering around two to six per frog each feeding. Clown tree frogs are particularly fond of flying insects, and relish both moths and houseflies, which can be offered regularly to vary their diet. *Drosophila hydei*, a larger species of flightless fruit fly, will also happily be devoured.

Breeding

Captive breeding is occasionally achieved. With an increase in temperature, humidity, and food availability, males begin to call loudly each night. If fed heavily, females will soon swell with eggs. Breeding can occur in their normal cage or in a rain chamber, with eggs being laid on the sides of water dishes, emergent vegetation, or leaves overhanging water. As many as 600 eggs are laid. The resulting tadpoles can be cared for in the usual way, being kept in water heated to a tropical temperature and fed fish flake until they metamorphose.

Marbled Tree Frog

The marbled tree frog (*Dendropsophus marmoratus*) is patterned in varying shades of white, tan, and gray. These colors are bordered in thin black lines, which outline their complex swirls and blotches.

With this pattern, the marbled tree frog effectively looks like a bird dropping when perched on a leaf or piece of bark. If this complex camouflage doesn't work well, and they are disturbed by a predator while sleeping, they quickly leap from their resting place, exposing the bright orange flash marks concealed on the insides of their legs, hopefully startling the predator long enough to make an escape.

Adults range in size from 1.6 to 2.2 inches (4.0 to 5.6 cm), with females being larger than males. They occur throughout the Amazon Basin, where they spend much of their time in trees, but also often descend to lower levels around temporary ponds formed after heavy rains.

Care

Easily kept and interestingly patterned, the marbled tree frog makes a good captive. Wild-caught adults are sporadically available, usually originating from Suriname. Occasionally, marbled tree frogs are bred in captivity, and it's preferable to acquire captive-bred individuals from a breeder than to get wild-caught adults. A group of five or six can be housed in a standard 20-gallon (76-l) aquarium. The setup, along with the temperature and humidity parameters, is similar to those described for the clown tree frog.

Marbled tree frogs are pigs and will gorge themselves on crickets, houseflies, and most other suitably sized feeders. They will quickly learn when it's feeding time and have no problem eating from the keeper's hand or waking up during the day to catch a meal that's on the move.

Breeding

Breeding takes place after heavy rains in the wild, around ponds and other bodies of water. Females can produce over 1,500 eggs in one clutch, so a single successful breeding in captivity can yield hundreds of baby marbled tree frogs. Induce breeding by feeding heavily and keeping the cage both warm and humid. Once the females look fat and the males are calling nightly, the frogs can be moved to a rain chamber. This should have several inches of water in the bottom, along with some floating vegetation or protruding rocks. Females deposit eggs on the surface of the water and, if they are fertile, tadpoles emerge in 1 or 2 days. Tadpoles grow quickly when kept warm and fed fish flake.

Marbled tree frog clinging to the terrarium glass. This is an excellent subject for a living terrarium.

Mexican Leaf Frog

The Mexican leaf frog (*Pachymedusa dacnicolor*) is a big-bodied frog, native to arid subtropical and tropical forests on the Pacific coast of Mexico. These forests are associated with an extended dry season, during which water is very limited. When rain finally arrives, Mexican leaf frogs breed en masse, congregating in large numbers around temporary bodies of water. They grow large, with females able to reach 3.9 inches (10 cm). Their dorsal coloration varies from lime green, to bluish turquoise, to a dirty olive color, and sometimes brown. Small white to gold spots are patterned over this on most individuals.

Care

Captive-bred Mexican leaf frogs are available from time to time and make outstanding captives. A standard 29-gallon (110-l) aquarium is large enough for two or three adults. A bare-bottom, paper towels, coconut husk fiber, or soil are all good substrates. Whichever you choose, it is important that it stays fairly dry. Furnishings can include cork bark, driftwood, PVC pipe perches, and artificial plants. If live plants are used, ensure they can support the hefty weight of a full-grown Mexican leaf frog. Also, offer a suitable water dish.

Over one end of the cage, a low-wattage incandescent light bulb should be placed. This can be turned on during the day to bring about an increase in temperature in one area, creating a temperature gradient. At night, this light should be turned off, allowing the cage to cool.

The usual variety of feeder insects will be eaten by Mexican leaf frogs. Crickets can make up the majority of their diet, with other food items being substituted for crickets every few feedings.

Breeding

Breeding takes place in the wild after a long dry season, and duplicating similar conditions in captivity is necessary to breed Mexican leaf frogs. After several weeks or months of dry captive conditions, mist the enclosure with water daily. In addition to increasing the humidity, increase the availability of food. Once males are calling and females look swollen with eggs, the frogs can be moved to a rain chamber. A couple hundred white eggs are laid on leaves and branches overhanging water. These and the resulting tadpoles can be cared for as described in the monkey frog chapter.

White-Lipped Tree Frog

Closely related to White's tree frog (Litoria caerulea), the white-lipped tree frog (L. infrafrenata) appears similar, but with a white stripe running around its lower lip and greener coloration. It also grows significantly larger and is capable of surpassing 5.0 inches (12.7 cm) in length. It inhabits humid forests and swamps in Papua New Guinea, eastern Indonesia and surrounding islands, as well as a small portion of Australia, northeast of Queensland.

The care of Mexican leaf frogs is similar to that of waxy monkey frogs.

L. infrafrenata is an impressive tree frog because of its large size and simple, but elegant appearance, and it can make a good captive. Unfortunately, they are not as docile or hardy as their relative, the

Good Terrarium Frogs

Their small size and tolerance of high humidity make both the clown tree frog and marbled tree frog excellent candidates for a living terrarium. The small leaves of plants such as the wandering Jew (*Tradescantia fluminensis*), or the tight axils of bromeliads are both used as resting spots during the day for captive clowns. Marbled tree frogs seem to prefer to rest on either cage objects, or on large, broad-leaved plants. Plant your terrarium appropriately to accommodate the specific frog that you plan to keep.

White's tree frog. Most white-lipped tree frogs available originate from the wild and, while being transported, sometimes develop parasite problems, infections, or injuries. It's therefore important to inspect individual frogs carefully before making a purchase and to keep a close eye on their health during acclimation.

Care

White-lipped tree frogs need a roomy, well-ventilated enclosure. This should be fitted with an assortment of perches and artificial plants. Being a large frog, the white-lipped tree frog also produces a large amount of waste, and they are best kept on a simple substrate to accommodate the necessary frequent cleanings. Keep them within a similar temperature range as that required by White's tree frog but with higher humidity. You may need to mist the cage with water once or twice a day to keep the humidity high. Provide a diet consisting largely of crickets. Every few feedings, other large food items like cockroaches, super worms, silkworms, and moths can be substituted for crickets.

Breeding

Breeding can be achieved by giving the frogs a one to two month artificial dry season, during which you only feed and mist them sparingly. Following this dry period, feed heavily multiple times each week and spray the cage with water a couple times a day. This should stimulate males to call, and at this point you can move the tree frogs to a rain chamber. It's been suggested that white-lipped tree frogs breed best when in a large group with multiple males.

White-lips lay their eggs on the surface of the water, with a single female capable of producing over 3,000 eggs. Remove frogs from the rain chamber if no eggs are found after one week. At a water temperature between 79°F (26°C) and 81°F (27°C), most tadpoles complete metamorphosis within six to eleven weeks. The resulting miniature white-lipped tree frogs only measure around 0.8 inches (2.0 cm), but grow quickly when fed plenty of

Newly metamorphosed Mexican leaf frog. Hobbyists breed this species in fairly good numbers.

fruit flies and appropriately-sized crickets. Cannibalism is not uncommon, so separate young frogs of different sizes into different enclosures to prevent smaller individuals from being eaten by their larger counterparts.

Golden Tree Frog

The golden tree frog (*Polypedates leucomystax*) has a large range in tropical Asia, where it inhabits forests, wetlands, and many human-made environments, such as gardens, drainage ditches, and houses. Large females may reach 3.5 inches (8.9 cm) in length, while males mature to a smaller size. They have angular heads and streamlined bodies, which can vary in color from solid orange, tan, or beige, to a striped brown and gray.

Care

Golden tree frogs do well in captivity, and are hardy when given appropriate conditions. They have a nervous disposition and will sometimes develop rostral abrasions if housed in enclosures that are too small. A standard 20-gallon (76-l) aquarium is large enough for a trio of frogs. In terms of temperature, humidity, and cage setup, offer conditions similar to those required by White's tree frog, but provide higher humidity levels. Golden tree frogs are not picky eaters and will consume the normal assortment of feeders, including crickets, roaches, houseflies, and food can be offered to adult frogs every 3 or 4 days.

Breeding

Breeding occurs periodically in captivity. They create a foam nest around their eggs, providing moisture and oxygen while the larvae develop inside. In the wild, this nest normally overhangs a body of water. Captive golden tree frogs will sometimes create their nest above the water dish in the

All the Same Frog

P. leucomystax is offered for sale under many common names, including golden tree frog, golden foam nest frog, golden flying frog, banana tree frog, common tree frog, and Asian tree frog.

terrarium, but they also may deposit the nest on the floor of the cage. In this circumstance, move the nest and suspend it over water. Heavy feedings and an increase in humidity and moisture encourage breeding behavior. Tadpoles hatch from the foam nest in 1 to 3 days and initially appear motionless. They will complete metamorphosis between 2 and 3 months, feeding well on fish flake and algae.

The care of white-lipped tree frogs is similar to that of White's tree frogs, but white-lips need higher humidity.

Reinwardt's Flying Frog

With webbing between their toes, Reinwardt's flying frog (*Rhacophorus reinwardtii*) is able to glide between trees with ease in the forests of tropical Asia. They spend much of their time high in the canopy, descending to breed on branches and leaves that overhang water. Their dorsum and heads are mainly green, which contrasts sharply with their orange flanks. A navy blue spot is present on the sides of their bodies, under their arms, and is more distinct in males. The enlarged feet and webbing of Reinwardt's flying frog are similarly colored in orange and navy blue. Adult females are larger than males, and are capable of reaching 3.1 inches (7.9 cm). Males normally mature between 1.6 (4.1 cm) and 2.1 inches (5.2 cm). Although highly desirable because of their attractive coloration, Reinwardt's flying frog is only suitable for a small handful of keepers. They are difficult to acclimate to captivity, and require a large, well-furnished cage.

Care

Reinwardt's flying frog is periodically available from dealers, breeders, and pet stores, sometimes being sold under other common names such as blue-webbed gliding frog or Java flying frog. Breeding infrequently occurs in captivity, but captive-bred frogs are worth searching for because those that arrive from the wild are notorious for acclimating poorly. Once established, however, they make good captives when provided with a large, natural enclosure that is kept clean.

These frogs are capable of jumping long distances, and sometimes injure themselves when kept in too small a cage. Their enclosure should therefore measure several feet (1m or more) in length and height. It must also be well-ventilated and fitted with an assortment of branching pieces of driftwood and broad-leaved plants for cover. A water dish should be provided and changed daily. Warm temperatures and high humidity are necessary for R. reinwardtii to do well, with a temperature around 80°F (27°C) or slightly warmer during the day being suitable. At night, allow the cage to cool. Mist their enclosure daily to ensure that the humidity level stays high. Reinwardt's flying frogs will feed well on the usual assortment of feeder insects.

Breeding

In their native forests of southeast Asia, Reinwardt's flying frog descends from high in the canopy during the rainy season to breed on vegetation that overhangs water. They breed en masse, with large numbers of frogs congregating at one time around one common body of water. It may be helpful to have a group of frogs in captivity to promote breeding behavior, particularly if there are multiple males in the group to compete for breeding rights.

Eggs are laid in a foam nest that prevents the eggs from desiccating. As tadpoles develop in the nest, they drop into the water below. It has been noted by at least one experienced frog keeper that captive-bred R. reinwardtii are not as brightly colored as those originating in the wild.

Big-Eyed Tree Frogs

The genus *Leptopelis* is diverse and contains around 50 species, all native to Africa. Some are fossorial and spend much of the year buried underground, while others fit the description of a tree frog well, having enlarged toe pads and an arboreal lifestyle.

Golden tree frogs range over much of Asia, from India to the Philippines and Indonesia.

Two arboreal *Leptopelis* species are imported regularly, with several others sporadically showing up here and there. Most common is *L. vermiculatus*, often found for sale under the common name peacock tree frog or Usumbara big-eyed tree frog. They are a large *Leptopelis* species, with females capable of reaching 3.3 inches (8.5 cm). Males stay smaller, to between 1.5 (3.9 cm) and 2.0 inches (5.0 cm). Juveniles are a beautiful emerald green color (as are most young *Leptopelis*), intricately patterned in tiny black markings. As they mature, some retain a similar coloration, while others change to a drab tan and brown.

Gliding Frogs

The Chinese gliding frog, *Rhacophorus (Polypedates) dennysi*, is a large-bodied, green tree frog native to southeast China, Vietnam, and Laos. Occasionally available, these robust amphibians require spacious enclosures because of their large size and active behavior. They also generate a large amount of waste, so they should be kept on a simple substrate that is easily cleaned. Chinese gliding frogs are quite tolerant of a range of environmental conditions, but are best kept within those conditions described for the golden tree frog (*P. leucomystax*) or White's tree frog (*L. caerulea*). When cared for in this way, they make excellent captives.

The ornate big-eyed tree frog, L. *flavomaculatus*, is also often available. They range in color from solid brown to green, normally with a large, dark, triangular marking in the middle of their backs. The larger female L. *flavomaculatus* can reach 2.8 inches (7.0 cm) in length. Additional species sometimes offered for sale include L. *argenteus*, L. *barbouri*, L. *boulengeri*, L. *brevirostris*, and L. *uluguruensis*.

Care

In captivity, some big-eyed tree frogs make hardy captives, while others are more sensitive. Both L. *flavomaculatus* and L. *vermiculatus* fit the first category well, but the keeper must acquire individuals in good health. Nearly all big-eyed tree frogs available are wild-caught, and their fate in captivity depends on their initial condition when acquired.

You can use a standard 15- or 20-gallon (57- or 76-L) aquarium to house up to four frogs. It should be furnished simply,

Reinwardt's flying frog requires a spacious enclosure to prevent stress and injuries.

with a paper towel or coconut husk fiber substrate, potted plant, piece of driftwood, and water dish. Maintain a temperature during the day that ranges from 75°F (24°C) to 85°F (29°C), allowing a nighttime drop down to around 68°F (20°C). High humidity is not required, although misting the cage lightly a few times a week is not a bad plan. Big-eyed tree frogs feed very well on crickets, with other feeders like houseflies and moths being substituted for crickets every couple weeks.

Reed Frogs

The common name of "reed frog" is usually used for the genus *Hyperolius*, which contains around 125 species of small, arboreal frogs that inhabit savannas, grasslands, and forests in sub-Saharan Africa. They spend the day exposed, sleeping on reeds or tall grasses surrounding ponds, drainage ditches, or other water sources. Many are patterned in attractive stripes or spots and are capable of changing color rather dramatically. As adults, most species mature to only around 1.0 inch (2.5 cm) in length. Species regularly encountered in the pet trade include the Argus reed frog (*H. argus*), painted reed frog (*H. marmoratus*), Mitchell's reed frog (*H. mitchelli*), Parker's reed frog (*H. parkeri*), tinker reed frog (*H. tuberilinguis*), and common reed frog (*H. viridiflavus*). The common name "reed frog" is also sometimes used for species of the genera *Afrixalus* and the Madagascar-endemic *Heterixalus*. Species of both can be cared for in much the same way as *Hyperolius* species.

Care

A group of seven or eight adult frogs can be kept in a standard 15-gallon (57-l) aquarium, lined with moist paper towels, coconut husk fiber, or sphagnum moss. Within the cage, it's important to provide supportive perches for them to rest on during the day. Bamboo poles, branching pieces of driftwood, and artificial or live plants can all be used. Captive reed frogs seem to particularly enjoy spending the day asleep in bromeliads or other plants with tight leaf axils. Because they do not grow large, reed frogs do well when kept in living terrariums. Use caution when opening a cage housing reed frogs. These little amphibians love to rest in the upper corners of aquariums, and they

Several species of *Leptopelis* show up in the hobby on occasion. The peacock tree frog (*L. vermiculatus*) (top) is probably the most common, while *L. uluguruensis* (bottom) is a rarity in the hobby.

Nesting Frogs

Many *Leptopelis* species breed by creating shallow nests in the ground. The well-adapted tadpoles use their specialized tail to wriggle out of the nest to nearby water. There is much to be learned about breeding big-eyed tree frogs in captivity, and it's worth experimenting to develop a suitable breeding setup to accommodate their unique reproductive behavior.

sometimes get spooked, resulting in a scared frog leaping out of the cage as the cover is removed.

Light intensity and temperature play a large role in the colors reed frogs display, so it's advantageous to use strong lighting over their enclosure. A couple of standard fluorescent tubes can be used for this purpose. In addition to these lights, a low-wattage incandescent bulb should be placed over one end of the cage to provide a warm spot above a branch or plant. The temperature in this area can approach 90°F (32°C), while the rest of the cage should remain cooler, between 70°F (21°C) and 80°F (27°C). Mist the cage as needed to maintain high levels of humidity.

For being such a small animal, reed frogs have huge appetites. They particularly enjoy chasing flying insects, so offer moths or houseflies on a regular basis. These can be used in addition to a diet of small crickets and flightless fruit flies.

Breeding

Wild reed frogs breed during the rainy season, and you can encourage captive frogs to breed by simulating similar environmental conditions. In cages where a large water dish is available, breeding will sometimes occur simply when reed frogs are well-fed and the humidity is high. Some people have also had success moving their reed frogs to small rain chambers. It's been suggested that they breed best when there are several competing males to each female. Small clumps eggs are deposited in, on, or above water, on vegetation, and total anywhere from 50 to 600 depending on species. Tadpoles are reported to be hardy, and feed well on algae-based fish foods. Newly metamorphosed reed frogs and juveniles often only display one of the possible patterns of the adult frog, changing as they mature into their adult form.

The painted reed frog is highly variable in color and pattern.

Abate, Ardi. *Thoughts for Food.* 3rd ed. Chameleon Information Network, 2002.

AmphibiaWeb. 2006. University of Berkeley California. 5 Feb. 2007 http://amphibiaweb.org/index.html.

Bertoluci, J, P.S. Santos, M.A.S. Canelas, and J. Cassimiro. "Phyllomedusa burmeisteri." *Reptilia* Apr 2005: 38-42.

Bertoluci, Jaime. "Pedal Luring in the Leaf-Frog Phyllomedusa burmeisteri." *Phyllomedusa* 1 (2002): 93-95.

Biggi, E. "Fairies of the Trees. Monkey Frogs of the Genus Phyllomedusa." *Reptilia* Apr. 2005: 10-21.

Biggi, E. "Phyllomedusa hypocondrialis azurea." *Reptilia* Apr. 2005: 22-30.

Capobianco, Henry. "Care Sheet for Low Land Leptopelidae." *Terra Typica.* 4 Feb. 2007 http://www.terra-typica.ch/berichte/Leptopelis/leptenglish.htm.

Channing, Alan. *Amphibians of Central and Southern Africa.* Ithaca, NY: Cornell UP, 2001.

Channing, Alan, and Kim Howell. *Amphibians of East Africa.* Ithaca, NY: Cornell UP, 2006.

Church, Gilbert. "The Variations of Dorsal Pattern in Rhacophorus leucomystax." *Copeia* 1963 (1963): 400-405.

Cooper, Steve. "Red-Eyed Wonders." *Reptiles* Mar. 2002: 28-35.

Coote, Jon. "Phyllomedusa sauvagii: the Pet Frog of the Future." *Reptilia* Feb. 1999: 64-68.

Erspamer, V, GF Erspamer, C Severini, RL Potenza, D Barra, G Mignogna, and A Bianchi. "Pharmacological Studies of 'Sapo' From the Frog Phyllomedusa bicolor Skin: a Drug Used by the Peruvian Matses Indians in Shamanic Hunting Practices." *Toxicon* 31 (1993): 1099-1111. 27 Jan. 2007 http://www.ncbi.nlm.nih.gov.

Faivovich, Julian, Celio Haddad, Paulo Garcia, Darrel Frost, Jonathan Campbell, and Ward Wheeler. *Systematic Review of the Frog Family Hylidae, with Special Reference to Hylinae: Phylogenetic Analysis and Taxonomic Revision.* American Museum of Natural History. New York, NY: Bulletin of the American Museum of Natural History, 2005.

Fenolio, D. 1998. Notes on the Captive Reproduction of the Amazonian Milk Frog (Phrynohyas resinifictrix). *Reptiles,* April 1998:84-89.

Fenolio, Danté. "Captive Reproduction of the Orange-Legged Monkey Frog (Phyllomedusa hypochondrialis), and the Development of a Protocol for Phyllomedusine Frog Reproduction in the Laboratory." *Advances in Herpetoculture.* Des Moines, Iowa: Crown Craft Printing, 1996. 13-21.

Frog Decline Reversal Project. 2006. "How to Recognise Chytrid Fungus." 3 Feb. 2007. http://www.fdrproject.org/pages/disease/CHYrecog.htm.

Frost, Darrel R. "Amphibian Species of the World: an Online Reference. Version 5.0." 1 Feb. 2007. American Museum of Natural History. 4 Feb. 2007 http://research.amnh.org/herpetology/amphibia/index.html.

IUCN, Conservation International, and NatureServe. 2006. Global Amphibian Assessment. 5 Feb. 2007. www.globalamphibians.org.

Jarvie, Michelle. "Toad-Talk and Frog-Speak: Male Chorusing and Female Sexual Selection in Anurans." 11 Dec. 2002. Michigan Technological University. 3 Feb. 2007 http://www.bio.mtu.edu/~mmjarvie/Evolution%20report.pdf#search=%22Polypedates%20leucomystax%20female%20call%22.

Kowalski, Edward. "They are What They Eat." *Reptiles* Aug. 2004: 40-43.

Kubicki, Brian. *Leaf-Frogs of Costa Rica.* 1st ed. INBio, 2004. 74-85.

Miller, Jessica J. "Rhacophorus reinwardtii." *Livingunderworld.org.* 5 Feb. 2007 http://www.livingunderworld.org/anura/database/rhacophoridae/rhacophorus/reinwardtii/.

Neckel-Oliveira, Selvino, and Milena Wachlevski. "Predation on the Arboreal Eggs of Three Species of Phyllomedusa in Central Amazônia." *Journal of Herpetology* 38 (2004): 244-248.

Ohler, Annemarie, and Magali Delorme. "Well Known Does Not Mean Well Studied: Morphological and Molecular Support for Existence of Sibling Species in the Javanese Gliding Frog Rhacophorus reinwardtii (Amphibia, Anura)." *Comptes Rendus Biologies* 329 (2006): 86-97.

Picken, Les. "Foam & Fortune—Foam Nest Frogs." *Reptile Care* Jan.-Feb. 2005: 53-57.

Picken, Les. "Thigh of the Tiger." *Reptile Care* Dec. 2004: 44-47.

Purser, P. "Chorus of the Night: Care and Maintenance of Five Popular Tree Frogs." *Reptilia* June 2003: 22-25.

Reynolds, Gail. "Flying Frogs." *Reptile Hobbyist* June 1997: 44-50.

Rodriguez, Lily O., and William E. Duellman. *Guide to the Frogs of the Iquitos Region, Amazonian Peru.* Lawrence, Kansas: The University of Kansas Natural History Museum, 1994.

Savage, Jay M. *The Amphibians and Reptiles of Costa Rica.* Chicago, IL: University of Chicago P, 2002. 281-283.

Schiesari, Luis, and Marcelo Gordo. "Treeholes as Calling, Breeding, and Developmental Sites for the Amazonian Canopy Frog, Phrynohyas resinifictrix (Hylidae)." *Copeia* (2003): 263-272.

Searcey, Rex L. "Meet the Reed Frogs." *Reptiles* Oct. 2001: 48-65.

Slavens, Frank. "Longevity—Frog & Toad Index." *Frank and Kate's Webpage.* 2003. 3 Feb. 2007 http://www.pondturtle.com/lfrog.html.

Soden, S. "Phyllomedusa bicolor—Breeding Giant Waxy Monkey Frogs." *Reptilia* Apr. 2005: 31-37.

Staniszewski, Marc. "Hylidae." *Reptilia* June 2003: 14-21.

Tuttle, James. *Blaberus.com.* 2004. 6 Feb. 2007. www.blaberus.com.

Vosjoli, Philippe de, Robert Mailoux, and Drew Ready. *Care and Breeding of Popular Tree Frogs.* Mission Viejo, CA: Advanced Vivarium Systems, 1996.

Vosjoli, Philippe de, Robert Mailoux, and David Travis. "Keeping and Breeding the Amazing Chacoan Monkey Frog." *The Vivarium* May-June 1997: 38-42.

Young, Bruce E., Simon N. Stuart, Janice S. Chanson, Neil A. Cox, and Timothy M. Boucher. *Disappearing Jewels: the Status of New World Amphibians.* Arlington, Virginia: NatureServe, 2004.

CLUBS And SOCIETIES

Amphibian, Reptile & Insect Association
Liz Price
23 Windmill Rd
Irthlingsborough
Wellingborough NN9 5RJ
England

American Society of Ichthyologists and Herpetologists
Maureen Donnelly, Secretary
Grice Marine Laboratory
Florida International University
Biological Sciences

11200 SW 8th St.
Miami, FL 33199
Telephone: (305) 348-1235
E-mail: asih@fiu.edu
www.asih.org

Society for the Study of Amphibians and Reptiles (SSAR)
Marion Preest, Secretary
The Claremont Colleges
925 N. Mills Ave.
Claremont, CA 91711
Telephone: 909-607-8014
E-mail: mpreest@jsd.claremont.edu
www.ssarherps.org

Veterinary Resources

Association of Reptile and Amphibian Veterinarians
P.O. Box 605
Chester Heights, PA 19017
Phone: 610-358-9530
Fax: 610-892-4813
E-mail: ARAVETS@aol.com
www.arav.org

Rescue And Adoption Services
ASPCA
424 East 92nd Street
New York, NY 10128-6801
Phone: (212) 876-7700
E-mail: information@aspca.org
www.aspca.org

Las Cruces Reptile Rescue
www.awesomereptiles.com/lcrr/rescueorgs.html
New England Amphibian and Reptile Rescue
www.nearr.com

Petfinder.com
www.petfinder.org

Reptile Rescue, Canada
http://www.reptilerescue.on.ca/

RSPCA (UK)
Wilberforce Way
Southwater
Horsham, West Sussex RH13 9RS
Telephone: 0870 3335 999
www.rspca.org.uk

WEB SITES

Amphibiancare.com (author's website)
www.amphibiancare.com/frogs/main.html

Amphibian Specialist Group
www.amphibians.org.

Center for North American Herpetology
www.naherpetolgy.org/

The Complete Treefrog Homepage
http://members.core.com/~treefrog/

Costa Rican Amphibian Research Center
www.cramphibian.com/

Herp Digest
www.herpdigest.org

Herp Station
http://www.petstation.com/herps.html

Kingsnake.com
http://www.kingsnake.com

Marc Staniszewski's Amphibian Information Centre
http://www.amphibian.co.uk/

Melissa Kaplan's Herp Care Collection
http://www.anapsid.org/

Reptile Forums
http://reptileforums.com/forums/

The Reptile Rooms
http://www.reptilerooms.org/

Savafrog.org
www.saveafrog.org

MAGAZINES

Reptile Care
Mulberry Publications, Ltd.
Suite 209 Wellington House
Butt Road, Colchester
Essex, CO3 3DA
United Kingdom

Reptiles **Magazine**
P.O. Box 6050
Mission Viejo, CA 92690
www.animalnetwork.com/reptiles

Reptilia **Magazine**
Salvador Mundi 2
Spain-08017 Barcelona
Subscripciones-subscriptions@reptilia.org

Photo Credits:

Randall Babb: 45, 49, 62

Marian Bacon: 1, 30, 32, 67, 79 (top), 105, and front cover

Bartlett: 40, 42, 54, 58, 66, 72, 79 (bottom), 85, 89, 100, 107 (bottom), 110, and back cover

Marius Burger: 120

Matthew Campbell: 96

David Dube: 56

Devin Edmonds: 17, 25, 26, 27, 28, 46, 47, 75, 76, 108, 112

Isabelle Francais: 61, 73

Paul Freed: 10, 39, 43, 53, 68, 69, 82, 90, 106, 115, 119 (top)

James E. Gerholdt: 20, 34

Michael Gilroy: 52

Ray Hunziker: 37

Barry Mansell: 64

Sean McKeown: 94

G. & C. Merker: 4, 7, 8, 11, 18, 35, 80, 83, 86, 87, 113, 118

Aaron Norman: 6, 14, 65, 70

Shutterstock: 116

Mark Smith: 78, 91, 107 (top), 117, 119 (bottom)

Michael Smoker: 48, 97

Karl H. Switak: 23, 92, 95, 102

John C. Tyson: 99